DK EYEWITNESS TOP 10 TRAVEL GUIDES

CHICAGO

ELAINE GLUSAC
ELISA KRONISH
ROBERTA SOTONOFF

Left *Nighthawks,* The Art Institute of Chicago Right View from Sears Tower

LONDON, NEW YORK,
MELBOURNE, MUNICH AND DELHI
www.dk.com

Produced by Departure Lounge, London

Reproduced by Colourscan, Singapore
Printed and bound in Italy by Graphicom

First American Edition, 2004
06 07 08 09 10 9 8 7 6 5 4 3 2 1

Published in the United States by
DK Publishing, Inc.,
375 Hudson Street, New York,
New York 10014

Reprinted with revisions 2006

**Copyright 2004, 2006 © Dorling
Kindersley Limited, London
A Penguin Company**

ISSN 1479-344X
ISBN 0-75660-031-6
ISBN 978-0-75660-031-0

Within each Top 10 list in this book, no
hierarchy of quality or popularity is implied.
All 10 are, in the editor's opinion, of
roughly equal merit.

Floors are referred to throughout in
accordance with British usage; ie the "first
floor" is the floor above ground level.

Contents

Chicago's Top 10

The information in this DK Eyewitness Top 10 Travel Guide is checked regularly.
Every effort has been made to ensure that this book is as up-to-date as possible at the time of
going to press. Some details, however, such as telephone numbers, opening hours, prices,
gallery hanging arrangements and travel information are liable to change. The publishers
cannot accept responsibility for any consequences arising from the use of this book, nor for
any material on third party websites, and cannot guarantee that any website address in this
book will be a suitable source of travel information. We value the views and suggestions of
our readers very highly. Please write to: Publisher, DK Eyewitness Travel Guides,
Dorling Kindersley, 80 Strand, London, Great Britain WC2R 0RL.

Left **Frontera Grill** Center **Buddy Guy's Legends** Right **Chicago Blues Festival**

Left **Wave Swinger, Navy Pier** Right **Baha'i Temple, Wilmette**

Key to abbreviations
Adm *admission charge payable* **Free** *no admission charge* **DA** *disabled access*

CHICAGO'S TOP 10

CHICAGO'S TOP 10

🔟 Chicago Highlights

Big-city sophistication combined with small-town hospitality create the perfect blend in this, the Midwest's largest city. Chicago's influential architecture, cuisine for every budget and taste, great shopping, diverse ethnic neighborhoods, and outstanding museums are reason enough for a visit. And the icing on the cake? The city boasts a lakefront and park system that are as beautiful as they are recreational.

1 The Art Institute of Chicago

This grande dame of Chicago's art scene features world-renowned collections. The ever-popular Impressionist section *(see pp8–11)* includes outstanding exhibits such as Renoir's *Acrobats at the Circus Fernando.*

2 Sears Tower & its Views

The city's skyscraping superlative is actually made up of nine tube-like sections. The views *(left)* are absolutely awesome: on a clear day, you can see up to 40 miles (64 km) from the 103rd-floor Skydeck *(see pp12–13).*

3 Field Museum

Delve into cultures and environments from ancient Egypt to modern Africa, via Midwestern wildlife, and the underground life of bugs. The Field also offers a closeup of the world's largest and most complete *Tyrannosaurus rex* skeleton, as well as many other fossils *(see pp14–15).*

4 Museum of Science & Industry

An enduring family favorite, this museum is the only building left from the 1893 World's Columbian Exposition. Exhibits emphasizing interactivity cover everything from space exploration to coal-mining, including the Walk-Through Heart and Silver Streak train, which visitors can climb aboard *(see pp16–19).*

5 Navy Pier

Once dilapidated, this Lake Michigan pier is now a bustling year-round playground for kids and adults alike, complete with a Ferris Wheel and carousel. In warm weather, take a boat tour or join the throngs that stroll along the pier and get some amazing city views *(see pp20–21).*

Grand Ⓜ

Lake Ⓜ

Washington Ⓜ
WEST WASHINGTON STREET
Ⓜ Washington

Downtown

Monroe Ⓜ

WEST ADAMS STREET
Ⓜ Quincy Jackson Ⓜ
WEST JACKSON BLVD

Library Ⓜ

LaSalle Ⓜ
WEST CONGRESS PARKWAY

WEST HARRISON STREET
Harrison Ⓜ

400 —— yards → 0 ← meters —— 400

6 John G. Shedd Aquarium

Chicago's amazing aquarium is located on the lakefront and is home to thousands of marine animals from big beluga whales to tiny seahorses. Get a fun, fish-eye view at the Oceanarium's underwater viewing galleries *(see pp22–3).*

7 Lincoln Park Zoo

It might not be the biggest, but it's one of the oldest zoos in the country and, after more than 100 years, still free. Kids love the hands-on Children's Zoo and Endangered Species Carousel *(see pp24–5)*.

8 Magnificent Mile

Chicago's premier shopping destination is a four-lane stretch of North Michigan Avenue. It also has historic significance, claiming two of only a few structures to survive the 1871 Great Chicago Fire *(see pp26–7)*.

9 University of Chicago

Opened in 1892, this private university is an important part of the southside Hyde Park neighborhood. Its public attractions include museums and galleries, and a Frank Lloyd Wright home *(see pp28–9)*.

10 Frank Lloyd Wright's Oak Park

Frank Lloyd Wright, creator of Prairie Style architecture, was based in this Chicago suburb for 20 years. His legacy is an "outdoor museum" of 25 buildings. Take a self-guided or guided tour of his creations and those of other Prairie Style architects *(see pp30–31)*.

→

🔟 The Art Institute of Chicago

Guarded by iconic lions, and up a flight of grand stone steps (a favorite local meeting place) is the Midwest's largest, and one of the USA's best art museums. Housed in a massive Beaux Arts edifice (and subsequently greatly expanded), the Institute has some 300,000 works from around the globe, and is famous for its Impressionist and Post-Impressionist works and blockbuster touring shows.

Main museum entrance

🍴 The Garden Restaurant is a lovely lunch stop. Alternatively, cross over to Cosi (116 S. Michigan Ave.) for great sandwiches.

🎫 Join a free, hour-long introductory tour. Meet in gallery 100 (1 or 2pm Sat–Thu)

Don't miss the reconstruction of the 1893 Stock Exchange Trading Room.

In summer, catch live jazz in the Garden Restaurant (4:30–7:30pm Thu)

- 111 S. Michigan Ave.
- Map L6 • El Station: Adams (Green, Orange, Purple, & Yellow lines) Monroe (Blue & Red lines) • 312-443-3600
- www.artic.edu • Open 10:30am–4:30pm Mon–Fri (to 8pm Tue); 10am–5pm Sat & Sun.
- Adm: adults $12; students, seniors and children 6 yrs and older $7; under 5 free; free adm on Tue • DA (at both entrances)

Top 10 Paintings

1. A Sunday on La Grande Jatte–1884
2. Acrobats at the Circus Fernando
3. At the Moulin Rouge
4. Stacks of Wheat series
5. Paris Street; Rainy Day
6. Nighthawks
7. The Bath
8. The Old Guitarist
9. The Herring Net
10. American Gothic

1 A Sunday on La Grande Jatte–1884
Massive and mesmerizing, this painting took Georges Seurat two years to complete. The scene *(below)* is created from dots of color, based on his study of optical theory, later known as pointillism.

2 Acrobats at the Circus Fernando
Children were often the subjects of Renoir's sunny paintings: this luminous 1879 work shows a circus owner's daughters taking a bow after their act.

3 At the Moulin Rouge
Unlike many of his fellow Impressionists who painted serene, often natural scenes, Toulouse-Lautrec was drawn to the exuberant night- and lowlife of Paris. This dramatic composition (1892) celebrates the famous Moulin Rouge cabaret *(above)*.

4 Stacks of Wheat series
From 1890–91, Monet painted 30 views of the haystacks that stood outside his house at Giverny in France. This museum has six of them, which illustrate the basic Impressionist doctrine of capturing fleeting moments in nature.

5 Paris Street; Rainy Day
Considered to be Gustave Caillebotte's masterpiece, this evocative 1877 view down a Parisian boulevard, with life-sized figures in the foreground, perfectly captures the gray and rainy scene.

Nighthawks
6 One of the best-known images in 20th-century American Art, this 1942 painting by Realist Edward Hopper has a melancholy quality. It cleverly depicts fluorescent lighting, at the time a recent introduction to US cities.

Columbus Dr. entrance

Michigan Ave. entrance

Key to Floorplan

	Ground Level
	Main Level
	Upper Level

The Child's Bath
7 The only American to exhibit in Paris with the Impressionists, Mary Cassatt is known for using then-unconventional techniques such as elevated vantage points. She often portrayed women and children as in this, her most famous painting (1892).

The Old Guitarist
8 A 22-year-old, struggling Picasso painted this tortured 1903 portrait during his Blue Period. This reflected his grief over a friend's suicide and was a precursor to his own style of Cubism.

The Herring Net
9 Winslow Homer honed his realist skills as an illustrator for magazine and later for the Union during the Civil War. After moving to Maine, he created a series of images, including this one (1885), depicting man's complex relationship with the sea.

American Gothic
10 Grant Wood borrowed from the detailed style of Flemish Renaissance art to create this much-parodied painting (1930). Though perceived by many as satirical, the painting *(left)* celebrates rural American values.

Museum Guide

The main entrance is on Michigan Avenue, and another, less busy one is on Columbus Drive. Only the ground level connects the museum's three buildings. Head straight to the upper level for the Impressionist and Post-Impressionist collections. Unlike several other Chicago museums, the Institute is open on Monday.

For more Chicago art galleries and museums See pp38–9

Left **Ritual figure, Amerindian Art** Center **Thorne Minature Rooms** Right **Exhibit, Textiles**

TOP 10 Collections

1 European Paintings

Arranged chronologically, and spanning the Middle Ages through 1950, this prodigious collection includes a significant array of Renaissance and Baroque art. However, its main draw is a body of nearly 400 Impressionist and Post-Impressionist paintings. Instrumental in its creation was Bertha Honoré Palmer who acquired over 40 Impressionist works (largely ignored in France at the time) for the 1893 World's Columbian Exposition.

2 American Arts

This impressive holding contains some 5,500 paintings and sculptures dating from the colonial period to 1950. In addition, paintings and works on paper are on loan from the Terra collection and there is a range of decorative arts, including furniture, glass, and ceramics from the 18th century

Vincent Van Gogh, *Self-portrait (1886–7)*, European Paintings

Floorplan

Columbus Drive Entrance

Michigan Ave Entrance

through to the present. The silver collection is especially noteworthy.

3 Architecture

Given the city's strong architectural heritage and focus, it is not surprising that Chicago's Art Institute boasts an architecture department, one of only a few in the US. Sketches and drawings are accessible to the public by appointment and changing public displays feature models, drawings, and architectural pieces, such as a stained-glass window by Frank Lloyd Wright.

4 Contemporary Art

This important and wide-ranging collection represents all the significant arts movements to emerge in Europe and America from 1950 to the present day. In addition to a strong body of Surrealist works, and notable paintings by Picasso, Matisse, and Kandinsky, it affords an interesting opportunity to see how American artists, such as Georgia O'Keeffe, interpreted and reinvented European Modernism.

For more on Modern Art in Chicago See pp79, 94–5, 101

5 Textiles

Dating back to 300 BC are over 16,000 textiles and 66,000 sample swatches originating from Asia, Africa, Europe, and the Americas. Examples of clothing, needlework, tapestries, and lace are all featured. The items are extremely fragile, so exhibits are changed frequently.

Frank Lloyd Wright art glass, Architecture

6 Asian Art

This sizeable collection covers 5,000 years and features Chinese ceramics and jades, Japanese screens, and Southeast Asian sculpture. The museum's assemblage of Japanese woodblock prints, such as *Courtesan* (c. 1710) by Kaigetsudo Anchi, is one of the finest outside Japan. Look out, too, for the rare early 14th-century scroll painting, *Legends of the Yuzu Nembutsu.*

7 African & Amerindian Art

A variety of artifacts, including sculptures, masks, ceramics, furniture, textiles, bead-, gold-, and metalwork, make up this relatively small, but interesting collection. Exhibits from both continents are arranged by region and culture: ceremonial and ritual objects are particularly intriguing.

Clematis, Arthur Rubloff paperweight

8 Arms & Armor

The Harding Collection of Arms and Armor is one of the largest in America. On permanent display are over 200 items related to the art of war including weapons, and complete and partial suits of armor for men – as well as horses. The items displayed originate from Europe, the United States, and the Middle East, and date from the 15th through the 19th centuries.

9 Arthur Rubloff Paperweight Collection

This fabulous and unusual assemblage numbers in excess of 1,400 paperweights, making it one of the largest of its kind in the world. It showcases colorful and exquisite examples from all periods, designs, and techniques. The paperweights mostly originate from 19th-century France, though some were made in America and the United Kingdom. Displays also reveal the secrets of how paperweights are made.

10 Thorne Miniature Rooms

Narcissa Ward Thorne, a Chicago art patron, combined her love of miniatures with her interest in interiors and decorative arts to create the 68 rooms in this unique Lilliputian installation. Some of the 1 inch:1 foot scale rooms are replicas of specific historic interiors, while others are period recreations, combining features copied from a variety of sites or based on illustrations and other records of period furniture.

For more on American Art See p81

Sears Tower & its Views

It might have lost the world's tallest building slot to Kuala Lumpur's Petronas Towers, thanks to their ornamental spires, but Sears Tower (center, left) is still the tallest if measuring the height from ground to roof – a staggering 1,450 ft (440 m). Designed by Chicago firm Skidmore, Owings & Merrill, the tower uses nine exterior frame tubes, avoiding the need for interior supports. On a windy day, workers on higher levels can feel the building sway and hear squeaking noises: you might experience the same thing from the 103rd-floor Skydeck, where on a good day, the 360-degree views – the main draw for visitors – are awesome.

Sears Tower

The tower has eight restaurants to choose from (open Mon–Fri).

Take an audio Sky Tour to get "inside" information on Chicago at the Skydeck's 16 viewing points.

Check visibility levels at the security desk before you wait in line for the Skydeck.

- 233 S. Wacker Dr. (note: entrance is on Jackson Blvd.)
- 312-875-9696
- Map J4
- www.theskydeck.com
- El Station: Quincy
- Open May–Sep: 10am–10pm daily; Oct–Apr: 10am–8pm daily
- Skydeck adm.: $10.95; children (3–11): $7.65; seniors: $8.75 • DA
- Marina City: 300 N. State St. • Soldier Field: 425 E. McFetridge Dr.
- United Center: 1901 W. Madison St.
- McCormick Place: 2301 S. Lakeshore Dr.

Top 10 Views

1. John Hancock Center
2. Grant Park
3. Soldier Field
4. Navy Pier
5. United Center
6. Marina Towers
7. Merchandise Mart
8. McCormick Place
9. Lake Michigan
10. Chicago River

1 John Hancock Center

The Sears Tower's North Side counterpart is this 100-story skyscraper *(right, center)*. It houses a retail area, offices, and apartments – as well as an open-air observatory on the 94th floor *(see p79)*.

2 Grant Park

Built entirely on landfill following the Great Chicago Fire *(see p34)* this 200-acre (81-ha) park *(right)* is the city's largest and the site of summer music festivals *(see p62)*.

3 Soldier Field

Home to the Chicago Bears football team *(see p51)* for over 30 years, the 1924-built lakeside stadium *(below)* recently saw the addition of a controversial 63,000-seat structure. Critics have likened it to a padded toilet seat.

Plan of Navy Pier

5 Musical Carousel

A quaint merry-go-round of 36 hand-painted horses and chariots located next to the Ferris Wheel replicates a similar ride installed on the Pier in the 1920s.

6 Ferris Wheel

It's hard to miss the Pier's 15-story Ferris Wheel. The slowly and continually revolving ride seats six passengers in each of its 40 enclosed cars. Daytime rides offer fine lake views, while evening rides show off the magical city lights.

7 Chicago Shakespeare Theater

This highly renowned theater aims to make the Bard accessible to the pleasure-seeking masses visiting Navy Pier. As well as Shakespearean standards, productions also include the "Short Shakespeare" series for younger audiences.

8 IMAX® Theater

The six-story, 80-ft- (24-m) wide flatscreen movie theater offers celluloid fare ranging from scientific documentaries to Disney features. Sound and vision headsets aid 3D movie enjoyment.

9 Amazing Chicago's Funhouse Maze

This mirror-filled, Chicago-themed walking maze leads you on a disorienting, 15-minute trip. Expect spinning lights, startling sound effects, and new perspectives on city sights.

10 Miniature Golf Course

Putt your way around the 18-holes of this mini-golf course at the base of the Ferris Wheel. Each hole features a miniature Chicago landmark obstacle giving this attraction a real sense of fun and character.

Orientation

It's best to get a cab or bus to Navy Pier. But if driving, arrive early since the 1000-plus parking spaces soon fill up. Once there, be sure to stop off at the information desk just inside the main entrance to pick up a schedule for details of the day's events, including performance times and locations for the resident comedy troupe, brass band, and a capella singing group.

Chicago's Top 10

TOP 10 John G. Shedd Aquarium

The eponymous John G. Shedd, president of Marshall Field's department store (see p74), donated this Beaux Arts aquarium to Chicago in 1929. One of the city's top attractions ever since, it houses some 19,000 marine animals representing 1,500 different species that include amphibians, fish, and aquatic mammals. The latter romp in the saltwater of the 1991-built glass-walled Oceanarium, which places an infinity pool in front of Lake Michigan to transporting effect.

The Oceanarium

🅾 Choose one of three dining options at the Shedd: the sit-down Soundings serves upscale fare with stellar lake views; the Bubble Net Food Court offers pizzas, sandwiches, and burgers; or you can brown bag it at one of the picnic tables.

🅒 Don't miss the Shedd's underwater viewing galleries.

Check out the Shedd's live jazz on Thursdays (5–10pm, adm $10) from June through August.

- 1200 S. Lake Shore Dr.
- Map M6
- 312-939-2438 • www. sheddaquarium.org • El station: Roosevelt (Green, Orange, & Red lines)
- Open summer (Memorial Day to Labor Day): 9am–6pm daily, (to 10pm Thu Jun–Aug); winter: 9am–5pm Mon–Fri, 9am–6pm Sat & Sun • Adm (including Wild Reef and Ocean-arium): $23; children (3–11) & seniors: $16
- DA

Top 10 Exhibits

1 Caribbean Coral Reef
2 Oceanarium
3 Wild Reef
4 Habitat Chats
5 Worldwide Fishes
6 MacArthur Gallery
7 Amazon Rising
8 Animal Enounters
9 Tide Pool Touch
10 Oceanarium Shows

1 Caribbean Coral Reef

This vibrant tropical tank contains glinting tarpon, bonnethead sharks, fluttering rays, and many other fish. A scuba diver hand-feeds them five times daily *(right)*, narrating his task via an underwater microphone.

2 Oceanarium

Underwater galleries afford incredible views of the likes of dolphins and beluga whales swimming through the Oceanarium's vast pool. It is bordered by rocky outcrops and towering pines in an amazing re-creation of the Pacific Northwest coast.

3 Wild Reef

Gain a daring diver's perspective of whitetip reef, blacktip reef, sand-bar, and wobbegong sharks. The massive Queensland grouper and fearsome Lionfish *(left)* happily hold their own amid the predator school.

4 Habitat Chats

Oceanarium staffers hold daily discussions about the beluga whales, sea otters, and gentoo and rockhopper penguins in their charge. Twice daily there are also chats cover-ing a changing roster of fish from the aquarium.

Worldwide Fishes

5 Themed tanks holding over 300 species of fish include Ocean Coasts, Tropical Waters, and Africa, Asia, and Australia. An Australian lungfish known as "Grandad" is a celebrated resident, having lived here since 1933.

```
    2
  4    10
  6
8     9
  1
  3   5
  7
```
Entrance
Underwater galleries

Aquarium Plan

MacArthur Gallery

6 This 3,600 sq ft (334 sq m) special exhibit gallery is located on the mezzanine level of the Oceanarium and features changing exhibits focused on aquatic animals.

Amazon Rising

7 Demonstrating the huge seasonal tides of the world's longest river, this exhibit presents a year in the life of the Amazon flood plain. Look out for the ferocious red-bellied piranha *(above)*.

Animal Enounters

8 Get up close and personal with Chilean rose tarantulas, African bullfrogs, and red-tailed boas in handler-controlled encounters, twice daily.

Tide Pool Touch

9 Here, staffers guide visitors through touch tanks that imitate the tide pools of the Pacific Northwest coast. Seize your chance to stroke a starfish or tickle an anemone. Check times on arrival.

Oceanarium Shows

10 Four or five times a day trainers put the belugas *(left)* and dolphins through their paces. Children are chosen from the audience to reward the animals' intrepid feats (such as tailwalking, and vocalizing) with tasty treats.

Aquarium Guide

If you're visiting the Wild Reef, make a note of the time slot you've been allocated. Then consult the day's event schedule – on the map you're given – to get the most out of your visit. Try to arrive 10–15 minutes early for an Oceanarium Show to get the best seats, and remember that the 20–30 minute Habitat Chats often follow the shows. There are special events for the little ones on Tuesdays – call for details.

Lincoln Park Zoo

Chicago's second most popular attraction after Navy Pier, this menagerie is not only one of the oldest zoos in the country but also one of the last not to charge admission. Established in 1868 with just a pair of swans, its age helps to account for how well integrated it is with the surrounding North Side community. While small compared to lots of top US zoos, it is a leading light for ape research, and its park setting, duck ponds, historic café, and landmark red barn endear it to all who visit.

Entrance, Lincoln Park Zoo

Check out the Mexican fare year round at the Park Place Café. In summer, grab a pizza at the historic Café Brauer, which also has a beer garden – rare in the usually alcohol-free Chicago parks.

Have any animal-related questions? If so, ask staffers at the "Discovery Carts" located all around the zoo.

- 2200 N. Cannon Drive
- Map F3
- 312-742-2000
- www.lpzoo.org
- CTA bus 151; 156
- Grounds open: 9am–6pm daily.
- Buildings open summer & fall: 10am–5pm daily (summer: to 6:30pm Sat, Sun & hols); winter: 10am– 4:30pm daily • Adm: free but $2 charge for Endangered Species Carousel
- Parking: $12 • DA

Top 10 Exhibits
1. Polar Bear Pool
2. Small Mammal-Reptile House
3. Regenstein African Journey
4. Endangered Species Carousel
5. Regenstein Center for African Apes
6. Bird House
7. Children's Zoo
8. Lion House
9. Sea Lion Pool
10. Farm in the Zoo presented by John Deere

1 Polar Bear Pool
The highlight of this recently remodeled pool is the underwater viewing window through which zoo-goers can spy the beautiful sibling bears pawing their way through the water *(below)*.

2 Small Mammal-Reptile House
Replicating the warm climes of South America, Asia, Africa, and Australia, this exhibit introduces the exotic worlds of animals such as snakes *(below)*.

3 Regenstein African Journey
Elephants, rhinos, hippos, giraffes, and wild dogs are among the many animals to roam this expansive exhibit. Begin your walking adventure and experience total immersion in the sights and sounds of the varied African landscape around you.

4 Endangered Species Carousel
Ride a wooden tiger or a bamboo-munching panda on this tent-topped merry-go-round devoted to almost 50 endangered species, many of which are represented in the zoo itself. Admission is charged for this attraction.

For information on the neighboring Lincoln Park Conservatory **See p86**

5 Regenstein Center for African Apes

Simulating the natural habitat of chimps and gorillas, this exhibit offers huge indoor, tri-level spaces rigged with lifelike trees and vines, as well as an outdoor yard for use in summer.

West Entrance

East Entrance

South Entrance

Lincoln Park Zoo Plan

6 Bird House

Here, a series of habitats showcase their native bird species. And a walk-through tropical aviary allows you to have a close encounter with 20 exotic and endangered species, such as the African fairy bluebird.

7 Children's Zoo

The staffers here encourage kids to touch and pet the animals – from creepy-crawly taran-tulas to the more familiar fox – amid habitats scaled to the junior set.

9 Sea Lion Pool

Despite the name, harbor and gray seals inhabit this pool. Watch them play at the pool's edge or through an under-ground viewing window. Try to catch the 2pm feeding session *(above)*.

8 Lion House

This 1912 structure stands out not only for its grand architecture but also the grand inhabitants. Many kinds of big cats, including Siberian Tigers, prowl – and roar – both inside the hall and in outdoor enclosures.

10 Farm in the Zoo presented by John Deere

Keeping city kids in touch with their Midwestern roots, this exhibit offers a daily roster of activities such as goat-milking, cow-feeding, and butter-churning, and the chance to see chicks being born.

Visitor Guide

Stop by the Gateway Pavilion, just inside the east gate, when you arrive at the zoo. There, you can pick up a free visitor guide to find out about feeding times and special events. Staff are on hand here to provide extra information about any new animal arrivals or exhibits. Parking facil-ities, lockers, strollers, and wheelchairs are also available there.

🔟 Magnificent Mile

This glitzy strip of stores and striking buildings runs for, you guessed it, about a mile (1.6 km), along North Michigan Avenue. A sharp developer came up with the "magnificent" moniker in 1947, and it has stuck ever since. Often known as the Mag Mile, it is home to big-guns department stores like Neiman Marcus, as well as high-end boutiques such as Tiffany & Co, and popular chain stores (Gap et al). The strip is at its best around Christmas when twinkling trimmings provide welcome relief from the often gray days.

North Michigan Ave. Bridge

🍴 Choose from a wide range of high-end, global, fast food at Foodlife food court in the mall at Water Tower Place.

🎭 The Pumping Station has a visitor center and a Hot Tix booth (open 7:30am–7pm daily) for reduced same-day theater tickets *(see p80)*.

• Map L2–3
• Visitor Information 312-642-3570
• www.themagnificent mile.com
• El Station: Grand/State; Chicago/State
• Water Tower Place Mall: 845 N. Michigan Ave., 312-440-3165, open 10am–7pm Mon–Sat, noon–6pm Sun
• Garrett Popcorn Shop: 670 N. Michigan Ave., 312-944-2630, opening hours vary

Top 10 Features

1. The Drake Hotel
2. John Hancock Center
3. Water Tower Place
4. Historic Water Tower & Pumping Station
5. American Girl Place
6. Hershey's Chicago
7. Garrett Popcorn Shop
8. Hotel Intercontinental
9. Tibune Tower
10. Wrigley Building

2 John Hancock Center

When this sleek 100-story building was built in 1970, it was the world's tallest. Exhilarating views of Chicago and beyond are afforded by the 94th-floor observatory and adjoining open-air area, the Skywalk *(see pp76–7)*.

1 The Drake Hotel

This elegant hotel became an instant glamor hot spot when it opened on New Year's Eve in 1920. Marilyn Monroe was among the many stars who have graced it with their presence. High tea in the lobby café is a real treat *(see p115)*.

3 Water Tower Place

Housing one of the city's busiest shopping malls, this multi-use complex is one of the world's tallest reinforced concrete buildings. Its 100-plus shops include branches of the Marshall Field's and Lord & Taylor department stores.

4 Historic Water Tower & Pumping Station

Dwarfed by the surrounding skyscrapers, these structures are among the few that survived the Great Fire of 1871. The water tower *(left)* now contains an art gallery, while the pumping station still functions and also houses a visitor center *(see p80)*.

5 American Girl Place

Eager girls and their loving moms swarm to this palace of little-girliness *(see p82)*, which all kind of merchandise from the popular American Girl doll range. Try the store café *(see p57)* or attend the surprisingly acclaimed musical performances.

Magnificent Mile Map

6 Hershey's Chicago

North America's largest chocolate manufacturer offers a themed retail experience in its Chicago store. Old favorites such as *Hershey's Reese's* and *Kit Kat* are on sale alongside the latest new products *(see p81)*.

7 Garrett Popcorn Shop

A Chicago fixture since 1949, this beloved popcorn shop seduces mind-boggling numbers of people, who snake through its huge lines to get their bag of caramel, cheese, buttered or plain.

8 Hotel Inter-Continental

Built in 1929 as a luxury club for the all-male Shrine association, this amazing hotel *(see p115)* reveals a range of flamboyant architectural styles in its public spaces. Take a self-guided tour to see the highlights, including the stunning swimming pool *(above)*.

9 Tribune Tower

The result of a design competition organized by the *Chicago Tribune* newspaper, this Gothic tower *(above, right)* is either adored or abhorred by locals. Either way, it's a dramatic Mag Mile landmark *(see p80)*.

10 Wrigley Building

The two towers of Wrigley headquarters add to Michigan Avenue's exciting skyline *(above left)*. At night, colored lights illuminate them, as they have done since the building opened in 1921 *(see p61)*.

Bridge to Success

Built in 1920 and named a city landmark one year later, the $16 million North Michigan Avenue bascule bridge was the first of its kind in the world. Its creation was instrumental in Chicago's northward expansion and it provided a fitting gateway to what would later become the city's main retail artery – the Mag Mile. Imposing sculptures at its corners represent Pioneers, Discoverers, Defense, and Regeneration.

TOP 10 University of Chicago

With Chicago's expansion in the late 19th century, a major university was the perfect addition to an array of new cultural institutions. Funded by oil magnate John D. Rockefeller, (who deemed it his best ever investment) the forward-thinking institution opened in 1892. Today, the university is one of the USA's most respected, boasting 78 Nobel prize winners as students, faculty, or researchers, as well as several on-campus attractions that are destinations in their own right.

Cobb Gate

🍴 Go for a deep-dish pizza at a Chicago favorite, Girodano's (5311 S. Blackstone Ave.).

🎵 Rockefeller memorial chapel's carillon is played Oct–Jun 6pm Mon–Fri, noon Sun, Jun–Sep, every Sun.

• 5801 S. Ellis Ave.
• 1-773-702-1234
• www.uchicago.edu
• Map E6
• El Station: 51st St; Garfield Park
• Bond Chapel: open 8am–4:45pm daily, Free,
• Smart Museum of Art: open 10am–4pm Tue–Fri (to 8pm Thu); 11am–5pm Sat & Sun, Jun–Sep, Free
• Cobb Hall: Renaissance society open 10am–5pm Tue-Fri, noon–5pm Sat & Sun, Free
• Rockefeller Memorial Chapel: open 8am–4pm daily (except during services), Free
• Regenstein Library: special collections exhibits open to the public 8:30am–4:45pm Mon–Fri, Sat 9am–12.45pm term-time, Free

Top 10 Features

1. Oriental Institute
2. Bond Chapel
3. Smart Museum of Art
4. Main Quadrangle
5. Robie House
6. Cobb Gate
7. Nuclear Energy
8. Rockefeller Memorial Chapel
9. Cobb Hall
10. Regenstein Library

1 Oriental Institute
The institute's amazing museum *(see p99)* has five galleries that showcase the history, art, and archaeology of the ancient Near East. Don't miss the Egyptian Gallery's towering 17-ft (5.2-m) statue of King Tutankhamun *(right)*.

2 Bond Chapel
Built in 1926, this small, ivy-covered chapel features exterior stone carvings of angels, imps, and Adam and Eve. Inside, stained-glass windows illustrate scenes from the New Testament *(below)*.

3 Smart Museum of Art
Magazine moguls David and Alfred Smart founded this museum in 1974. It might be small, but its contents (ranging from ancient ceramics to 20th-century sculpture) pack an impressive punch.

4 Main Quadrangle
Rejecting post-Civil War modernity, Henry Ives Cobb's 1891 campus plan mimics England's Gothic Oxford University, with this main unifying quad surrounded by smaller ones.

Smart Museum of Art **3**
GREENWOOD AVENUE
EAST 56TH STREET
Nuclear Energy Sculpture **7**
ELLIS
10 Regenstein Library
EAST 57TH STREET
6 Cobb Gate
AVENUE
MAIN QUADRANGLE **4**
9 Cobb Hall
2 Bond Chapel
EAST 59TH STREET
Midway Plaisance
NORTH PLAISANCE

➡ *Unless otherwise stated, all attractions have Disabled Access.*

Robie House
5 Frank Lloyd Wright described his striking low-rise, Prairie-style masterpiece as "the cornerstone of modern architecture." The not-so-humble architect built it in 1909 for bicycle manufacturer Frederick C. Robie *(see p100)*.

Cobb Gate
6 This ornate northern entrance to the Main Quad is adorned with gargoyles. University lore says they represent students' four years of college life: from struggling freshman at the base to graduation at the apex.

Nuclear Energy
7 This 12-ft (3.65-m) bulbous bronze sculpture by Henry Moore marks the general area where Enrico Fermi and his team of scientists achieved the first controlled self-sustaining nuclear chain reaction in 1942.

Cobb Hall
9 Confusingly, the oldest building on campus is not named for its architect, Henry Cobb, but for an unrelated donor, Silas Cobb. Built in 1882, the beautiful Gothic structure houses classrooms, offices, and the Renaissance Society, a contemporary art gallery.

Robie House 5
EAST 58TH STREET
1 Oriental Institute
8 Rockefeller Memorial Chapel

UNIVERSITY WOODLAWN AVENUE

100 — yards ⌐0⌐ meters —100

Rockefeller Memorial Chapel
8 The tallest building on campus is this mini-cathedral named for university patron John D. Rockefeller. It boasts magnificent stained glass, a 72-bell carillon (the world's second largest), and a 10,000-pipe organ.

Top 10 Alumni
1. John Ashcroft (1942–), US Attorney General
2. Edwin Hubble (1889–1953), astronomer
3. Susan Sontag (1933–) critic/author
4. Eliot Ness (1903–57), author/law enforcer
5. George Stigler (1911–91) economist
6. Philip Roth (1933–), author
7. Carl Sagan (1934–96), astronomer/author
8. James D. Watson, (1928–), scientist
9. Philip Glass (1937–) composer/musician
10. Studs Terkel (1912–) oral historian

Regenstein Library
10 The 1970-built limestone "Reg," *(above)* honors Chicago industrialist Joseph Regenstein. Exceptional jazz archives, map collections, and children's books feature among its seven million plus volumes.

TOP 10 Frank Lloyd Wright's Oak Park

This quiet suburb, seven miles (11 km) west of downtown Chicago, contains the world's largest collection of Frank Lloyd Wright-designed buildings. It was here that Wright developed his Prairie style, (inspired by the flat lines of the Midwestern plains), influencing other architects such as George Maher. His work was first considered radical, even ugly, compared to the typical styles of the day. Walking through Oak Park's quaint, tree-lined streets, it's evident that Wright's unique architecture does stand out from the norm – but in all the right ways.

Detail of house in Oak Park designed by Wright

🍴 Dine Italian at family-run La Bella Pasteria (109 S. Marion St., 1-708-524-0044)

🎟 The Visitors' Center sells maps, books, and tickets for area tours (158 N. Forest Ave., 1-708-848-1500)

• Map A5
• El Station: Oak Park
• Frank Lloyd Wright Home & Studio, 951 Chicago Avenue, 1-708-848-1976, www.wrightplus.org, tours by appointment only, no DA
• Unity Temple, 875 West Lake Street
• Pleasant Home, 217 South Home Avenue
• Arthur Heurtley House, 318 Forest Avenue
• The Bootleg Houses, 1019/1027/1031 Chicago Avenue
• Charles Matthews House, 432 North Kenilworth Avenue
• Edwin Cheney House, 520 North East Avenue
• Beachy House, 238 Forest Avenue
• Nathan Moore House, 333 Forest Avenue
• Harry Adams House, 710 Augusta Boulevard

Top 10 Buildings

1. Unity Temple
2. Frank Lloyd Wright Home & Studio
3. Pleasant Home
4. Arthur Heurtley House
5. Beachy House
6. Charles Matthews House
7. Edwin Cheney House
8. The Bootleg Houses
9. Nathan Moore House
10. Harry Adams House

1 Unity Temple

This compact church (1908) wonderfully demonstrates Wright's use of poured concrete for both structural and decorative purposes *(right)*.

2 Frank Lloyd Wright Home & Studio

Built when Wright moved to Oak Park (1889), this is where he designed over 150 structures *(above)*. The children's playroom is luminous with signature art-glass windows.

3 Pleasant Home

This 30-room Prairie-style 1897 home built by George Maher, was Oak Park's first to have electricity. It holds a small history museum, including exhibits relating to Tarzan creator and former local resident, Edgar Rice Burroughs.

4 Arthur Heurtley House

Wright's beautiful 1902 house *(above)* is absolute Prairie, with its low, wide chimney, and band of art-glass windows that makes the over-hanging roof appear to float.

For detailed information on opening hours call the Visitors' Center. Most buildings open to the public are visited by tour only.

5 Beachy House

An impressive 1906 home that contradicts many of Wright's trademarks. Instead of just stucco and wood or brick and concrete, he used them all: it also has a seven-gabled, rather than a hipped, roof.

Oak Park Street Map

6 Charles Matthews House

Architects Thomas Eddy Tallmadge and Vernon S. Watson designed this elegant 1909 Prairie-style residence for a wealthy druggist. Among the interior details are Prairie-inspired light fixtures and folding art-glass doors.

7 Edwin Cheney House

Now a B&B, this home sparked a tragic love affair between Wright and Mrs. Cheney, leading him to abandon his family and practice. Mamah Cheney and her children were murdered at Wright's Wisconsin home by an insane servant in 1914.

8 The Bootleg Houses

Wright lost his job over these three private commissions, built while he was actually employed by Louis Sullivan (see p37). Though Queen Anne-like in style, they hint at the design elements that were to be his hallmarks.

9 Nathan Moore House

Out of financial desperation, Wright built this charming Tudor-style home (above) for his neighbor. After a fire destroyed the top floors in 1922, Wright's modifications echoed his West Coast concrete block houses.

10 Harry Adams House

This striking 1913 home marks the last of Wright's Oak Park houses and features several of the elements that made him famous, such as exquisite stained glass, and a low overhanging roof.

Frank Lloyd Wright

After moving to Oak Park in 1889, Wright (1867–1959) appeared to lead the perfect suburban life. But in the early 20th century he created scandals by galavanting with married women, and wearing flamboyant clothes and long hair. During the Depression, however, he transformed into a respected social visionary, and later redefined himself as a quick-witted sage. Ultimately, though, he became a master of self-promotion, establishing himself as the first celebrity architect.

For more information on places of interest see pp44–5 Frank Lloyd Wright's Oak Park birthplace is open to the public (339 N. Oak Park Ave., 1-708-848-2222)

Great Chicago Fire of 1871

🔟 Moments in Chicago History

1 **1871: Great Chicago Fire**
Over 250 people died and 17,000 buildings were destroyed in this fire, allegedly started by a cow kicking over a lantern. Just a few buildings survived, including the Historic Water Tower and Pumping Station (see p80).

2 **1885: First Skyscraper**
Though just a measly – by today's standards – nine stories, the Home Insurance Building (now demolished) was the tallest of its time. William LeBarron Jenney achieved this architectural feat by designing the first weight-bearing steel frame. From then on, the only way was up.

3 **1886: Haymarket Riot**
Wealthy industrialists funded amazing Chicago arts institutions, but their workers toiled long hours in abominable conditions. In May 1886, a labor protest ended in an explosion at Haymarket Square that killed eight policemen and two bystanders. Eight anarchists were convicted of murder, though three were later pardoned for lack of evidence.

4 **1892: First Elevated Train**
The first train traveled just 3.6 miles (5.8 km) along tracks built above city-owned alleys, (avoiding the need to negotiate with private property owners). By 1893, the line was extended to Jackson Park (see p62) to transport visitors to the World's Columbian Exposition (see p19).

5 **1900: Reversal of the Chicago River**
With sewage flowing downriver to Lake Michigan, the source of the city's drinking water, thousands of Chicagoans were dying from the contamination. To solve the problem, engineers created a canal that forced the river to flow away from the lake: an extraordinary feat of modern engineering.

Al Capone

6 **1919: Chicago Black Sox Scandal**
The Chicago White Sox was a winning baseball team but poorly paid, so players sometimes fixed games, pocketing money from gamblers. After a group of players conspired to lose the 1919 World Series, eight of them were indicted, acquitted for insufficient evidence, but banned for life from baseball – and forever nicknamed the "Black Sox."

7 **1929: Valentine's Day Massacre**
This brutal murder of seven of Al Capone's rival gangsters is one of history's most notorious massacres. Capone set up a sting that sent George "Bugsy" Moran's main men to a nearby garage. There, Capone's henchmen, dressed as police officers,

The Chicago White Sox in 1919

lined them up and riddled them
with bullets. Seven bushes now
mark the spot (at Clark Street
and Dickens Avenue).

8 1942: First atom split
Under the football stands on
the campus of the University of
Chicago *(see pp28–9)* Enrico
Fermi made history. He super-
vised the creation of a primitive
nuclear reactor and took the first
major step in understanding how
to build an atomic bomb.

9 1955: First McDonald's franchise opens
Ray Kroc, a milkshake mixer
salesman, changed diets world-
wide by convincing Dick and Mac
McDonald's to franchise their San
Bernadino, California burger stand.
The original restaurant in Des
Plaines – 15 miles (24 km) west
of Chicago – is now a museum.

10 1983: Harold Washington elected Mayor
Chicago's first African-American
Mayor, Washington tragically
died of a heart attack shortly into
his second term. His accomplish-
ments included the expansion of
O'Hare International Airport and
the creation of a new central
library *(see p69)*.

Top 10 Residents

1 Jean Baptiste Point du Sable
Chicago's first non-native
settler was an African-
American trader who set
up camp around 1779.

2 Jane Addams
This social activist (1860–
1935) founded Hull House
social center *(see p95)* and
won a Nobel Peace Prize.

3 Carl Sandburg
One of Chicago's
nicknames "City of big
shoulders," was penned by
this author/poet (1878–1967).

4 Al Capone
America's best-known
mobster (1899–1947) was
Chicago's "Public Enemy
Number One" until jailed in
1931 for tax evasion.

5 Ernest Hemingway
Born in Oak Park, this hard-
living author (1899–1947) left
the suburb of "wide lawns
and narrow minds" at age 19.

6 Richard J. Daley
This effective, if corrupt,
Chicago mayor (1902–76)
served longer than any other.

7 Benny Goodman
Born to poor Russian-
Jewish immigrants, jazz great
Goodman (1909–86) earned the
title "King of Swing."

8 Hugh Hefner
Lothario and founder of
Playboy (1926–), whose first
issue sold over 50,000 copies.

9 Curtis Mayfield
Soul musician and social
activist (1942–99), Mayfield had
his first hit *For Your Precious
Love* at age 17.

10 Oprah Winfrey
TV's talk-show darling
(1954–) has filmed in Chicago
since 1984 and become an
honorary native of the city.

Left **333 W. Wacker Drive** Center **Art glass, Auditorium Theatre** Right **860–80 N. Lakeshore Drive**

10 Skyscrapers

1 The Rookery
One of the earliest remaining skyscrapers, this 1888 Chicago landmark *(see p70)* combines traditional wall-bearing and newer steel frame construction. The latter made it possible for its architects, Burnham and Root, to design an open interior, with office spaces set around a central light well.

2 Auditorium Theatre
Built by Adler and Sullivan in 1889, the ornate Auditorium also originally contained a hotel and office building and had one of the first public air-conditioning systems. The revamped 4,000-seat theater boasts near-perfect acoustics. ✪ *50 E.Congress Pkwy.• Map K5 • For tours call 312-431-2354*

3 Monadnock Building
Constructed in two stages, this Loop edifice represents the evolution of skyscraper architecture. The northern half was built in 1891 using solely wall-

Detail of staircase, Monadnock Building

bearing construction, while the southern half was built two years later and incorporated the then emerging steel-frame technology that is still used today *(see p72)*.

4 Reliance Building
The steel skeleton on this 1895-built skyscraper allowed it to be wrapped in glass. It offers an excellent example of the Chicago window, which is characterized by a bay window placed between two narrow, double-hung windows – a signature feature of the Chicago school of architecture. Occupied by the Hotel Burnham *(see p116)* the interior sports replicas of original features *(see p72)*.

5 860–80 N. Lakeshore Drive
You might think these two highrise apartment buildings (1949–51) look like many others along this tony strip. Actually, the others look like these. German architect Mies van der Rohe perfected the "less is more" approach which so many other architects went on to copy.

6 Marina City
With its twin cylindrical structures (1964–7) on the Chicago River, Marina City is a "city within a city," containing offices, residences, a theater, a grocery store, and more. The apartments start on the 21st floor, affording spectacular views, but their slice-of-pie shape creates some interior decorating challenges.

The Rookery

Top 10 Architects

1 William Le Baron Jenney
The "father of the skyscraper" (1832–1907) who designed the first all-metal-framed structure in 1885 (see p34).

2 Daniel Burnham
Visionary city planner and architect, Burnham (1846–1912) was the man behind the White City (see p19).

3 William Holabird & Martin Roche
This influential team (Holabird 1854–1923; Roche 1855–1927) developed early Chicago-style skyscrapers including the Marquette Building (see p72).

4 Louis H. Sullivan
The creator (1856–1924) of the "form follows function" doctrine designed according to a building's intended use.

5 Frank Lloyd Wright
Inspired by the wide open spaces of the Midwest, Wright (see pp30–31) was the originator of the Prairie style.

6 George Maher
A Prairie School architect (1864–1926) who favored Arts and Crafts motifs.

7 Walter Burley Griffin
Another Prairie–style architect (1876–1937) with a namesake historic district on Chicago's Southside.

8 Ludwig Mies van der Rohe
Minimalist architect (1886–1969) and creator of the modern glass-and-steel box.

9 Bertrand Goldberg
A pupil of Mies van der Rohe who rebelled to produce curvilinear concrete shapes.

10 Harry Weese
A Modernist (1915–98), but one sympathetic to existing buildings of merit.

7 Sears Tower
This soaring tower, built in 1974 as the headquarters of retailer Sears Roebuck and Co. (who have since moved out), can be seen from almost anywhere in the city. Its Skydeck affords sensational views (see pp12–13).

8 333 W. Wacker Drive
The graceful curve of this triangular, tinted-glass office building (1983) hugs the Chicago River. The water, together with the changing light and clouds create dynamic reflections: the green and silver lobby continues the shimmering show. ⊗ Map K3

9 James R. Thompson Center
From inside the circular atrium of this magnificent 17-story building (1985), a quick glance up is almost dizzying. Take the elevator to the top for an impressive view of the stunning marble rosette on the concourse level (see p70).

10 Ogilvie Transportation Center
Rising 40 stories in waves of glass and steel is this striking 1996-rebuilt commuter train station (aka the Northwestern Station). Its streamlined façade mimics a vintage luxury train. ⊗ 500 W. Madison St. • Map J4

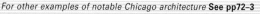

For other examples of notable Chicago architecture See pp72–3

Left **Exhibit, National Vietnam Veterans Art Museum** Right **Jane Addams Hull House**

TOP 10 Niche Museums

1 Mexican Fine Arts Center Museum

The largest Latino museum in the US explores the culture *sin fronteras* (without boundaries), showcasing works from both Mexico and Mexican-American communities. Pre-Columbian ceramics, Day of the Dead candelabras, and prints by such luminaries as Diego Rivera are highlights of the permanent collection. ◉ *1852 W. 19th St • Map B5 • 10am–5pm Tue–Sun • Free • DA*

2 Museum of Broadcast Communications

Dedicated to the culture and history of news and entertainment media, this museum archives over 70,000 radio and television programs and commercials. In addition to watching and hearing vintage tapes, visitors can anchor their own newscast and read from a teleprompter. ◉ *At State and Kinzie Streets • Map K3 • Open late spring 2006 • DA*

Exhibit, Museum of Broadcast Communications

3 Swedish–American Museum Center

Located in Andersonville, the historic neighborhood of Scandinavian immigrants, this tiny museum's permanent collection of personal items brought over by early settlers is supplemented by temporary exhibitions on Swedish culture. An interactive children's museum on the third floor brings the immigrant journey to life. ◉ *5211 N. Clark St. • Map K2 • 10am–4pm Tue–Fri, 11am–4pm Sat & Sun • Adm. • DA*

4 Museum of Holography

The art really jumps out at you in this quirky loft devoted to all kinds of laser-produced 3-D images. Exhibits relating to the technology employed explain how holographs are produced. ◉ *1134 W. Washington St. • Map J4 • 12:30pm–4:30pm Wed–Sun • Adm. • DA*

5 The Peace Museum

Art, history, and politics as seen through a pacifist's prism: the Peace Museum houses a 10,000-item collection, including sculpture, banners, and lithographs. Rotating exhibits cover themes such as 20th-century peace movements, the AIDS quilt, and art from Japanese A-bomb survivors. ◉ *100 N. Central Park Ave. • Map B5 • 11am–4pm,Thu–Sat, 1pm–4pm Sun, and by appt • Donation • No DA*

Work by Jesus Helguera, Mexican Fine Arts Center Museum

Hope and Help, International Museum of Surgical Science

6 Spertus Museum

Here, Judaica in forms ranging from cartoons to ancient Torah scrolls comprise a lively, multi-faceted retelling of Jewish history and culture. The museum's Zell Holocaust Memorial was the first such permanent installation in the US, while the Artifact Center gets kids involved in unearthing the past in a hands-on "archeological dig". ◊ *618 S. Michigan Ave.* • *Map L6* • *10am–5pm Sun–Thu (to 7pm Thu), 10am–3pm Fri* • *Adm., Free Fri* • *DA*

7 DuSable Museum of African-American History

Named for Jean Baptiste Point du Sable, Chicago's first settler (who was of African descent), this museum chronicles the African-American experience. There is a powerful exhibit on slavery, complete with shackles, while temporary displays cover topics such as early black millionaires, African hair art, and the *Kwanzaa* holiday celebration *(see p99).*

8 International Museum of Surgical Science

Medicine meets the macabre at this museum, with four floors displaying historic instruments that span 4,000 years of surgery. Murals and sculptures pay tribute to the honorable profession. Stronger stomachs may appreciate the ancient Peruvian skulls showing evidence of early surgical attempts. ◊ *1524 N. Lake Shore Dr.* • *Map F4* • *10am–4pm Tue–Sat May–Sep* • *Adm., Free Tue* • *DA*

9 National Vietnam Veterans Art Museum

Veterans of the Vietnam War, both US and Vietnamese, have contributed to the vast and moving collection of artworks cataloged by this thought-provoking museum. Some 130 artists created 1,000 works in pen, paint, clay, and word testifying to the horrors of war *(see p94).*

10 Jane Addams Hull House

Nobel Peace Prize-winning social reformer Jane Addams worked her good on Chicago's immigrant population from these two Victorian houses. In addition to her original art and furniture, Hull House stages temporary exhibits relating to the social settlement that brought day care, counseling, and education to the working class *(see p95).*

Left **Lou Mitchell's** Right **Blackbird**

🔟 Places to Eat

1 Charlie Trotter's
One of Chicago's top gourmet eateries, and one of the nation's best, Charlie Trotter's serves the exquisite and rarefied fare of its eponymous chef. The menu changes daily but expect creations such as venison loin with semolina cake, braised kale, and Niçoise olive *boudin*. Reservations must be made many weeks in advance though a last-minute call often turns up a table due to cancellations *(see p91)*.

2 Ambria
With its Art Nouveau detailing, cozy leather banquettes, and dark woods, Ambria is among the city's most romantic dining options. And the dining experience matches the style here as chef Gabino Soltelino prepares contemporary French meals with a sophisticated understatement. Service is formal and the sommelier is one of the best in Chicago *(see p91)*.

3 Gibson's Steakhouse
Boisterous and convivial, Gibson's exudes a good time. A regular crowd of politicians, sports figures, and conventioneers packs the place nightly. The steakhouse fare is in every way a match to the atmosphere – big and bold. Huge lobster tails vie for attention with large slabs of beef. A reservation is critical, but for a more casual, walk-in

Deep Dish Pizza, Pizzeria Uno

experience try the burgers next door at Hugo's Frog Bar.
🄫 1028 N. Rush St. • Map L2 • 312-266-8999 • $$$$

4 Blackbird
Foodies and the fashion set both agree on Blackbird, an eatery that sports minimalist decor and shoves the tables so close together that eavesdropping becomes part of the experience. Chef Paul Kahan generates the buzz, preparing sophisticated American dishes with French leanings. Menus change seasonally but reservations are perennially a must. 🄫 619 W. Randolph St. • Map J4 • 312-715-0708 • Lunch Mon–Fri, closed Sun • $$$$

5 North Pond Café
Hidden from the road in leafy Lincoln Park, North Pond is a treasure – once you find it. Lodged in an Arts-and-Crafts-style building, the café offers a seasonal menu with an emphasis on produce sourced in the Midwest. Though dinner is the star, lunches of sandwiches, soups, and salads are equally creative and well presented *(see p91)*.

6 Spring
Spring brings the sort of fine cooking you'd expect only to find downtown out to Northside's bohemian Wicker Park. Occupying a former bathhouse, the sunken feng-shui-inspired interior

Left **Museum of Science & Industry** Right **Visitors viewing animals, Lincoln Park Zoo**

Kids' Chicago

1 Chicago Children's Museum

The engrossing, imaginative exhibits here emphasize doing – be it digging up a dinosaur bone or designing a water channel. A central, three-story rope tunnel immediately snares the attention of older visitors, though there are age-appropriate attractions for infants to pre-teens. If this place can't exhaust the younger set's energies, nowhere can. ⊙ *700 E. Grand Ave. • Map L3 • Open 10am–5pm Tue–Sun (to 8pm Thu) • www.chichildrensmuseum.org • Adm.*

2 Lincoln Park Zoo

Free admission encourages repeat visits to the Lincoln Park Zoo *(see pp24–5)*. Many exhibits, including the working Farm in the Zoo and the Children's Zoo, allow kids to pet the animals. In summer a motorized "train" makes a scenic loop around the park, while on the pond, swan-shaped paddleboats float among the ducks.

Shedd Aquarium

3 Navy Pier

Kids make a beeline for Navy Pier's old-fashioned carnival rides including a 10-story Ferris Wheel and musical carousel . The ships that line the docks, from sleek, tall-masted schooners to powerful motor boats will also grab their attention. All the restaurants here are family friendly, and even the sculptures that line the Pier in summer are designed to with-stand climbers *(see pp20–21)*.

4 Elevated Trains

Chicago's elevated trains (the El) provide an inexpensive roofline tour of the city. The Brown Line in particular warrants riding en famille from Chicago Station south over the Chicago River and around the Loop, threading between the massive buildings of the financial district. Sit in the first row of the front car for an exciting view of the city ahead of you *(see p108)*.

5 Shedd Aquarium

Upon arrival, head straight for the Oceanarium to watch the thrilling dolphin and beluga whale show. Staff trainers frequently choose children in the audience to help them reward the marine mammals with a snack after each trick. At the daily Tide Pool Touch and reptilian Animal Encounters kids can indulge their urge to lay hands on the critters *(see pp22–3)*.

6 Westfield North Bridge Mall

Level 3 of this tony Michigan Avenue mall is primarily devoted to children's retailers including clothiers Oilily Children, Benetton Kids, The Children's Place, and

Unless otherwise stated, all attractions have Disabled Access.

Little Italy

the real Little Italy. It has a handful of authentic Italian restaurants and delis, as well as the Taste of Italy festival, held over Father's Day weekend every June. Map B5

7 Chinatown

An ornate arched gateway at Wentworth Avenue signals your entrance to this distinctly Chinese neighborhood. Asians and non-Asians alike flock to aroma-filled dim-sum restaurants that serve a mouthwatering selection of dumplings, duck, egg rolls, and other delicacies. Shops sell everything from lanterns to delicate tea sets and mysterious Chinese herbs (see p94).

8 Uptown

The eclectic Uptown neighborhood is nicknamed the United Nations for its ethnic diversity. Along Argyle Street, it's called Little Saigon for its predominantly Vietnamese flavor. Inexpensive restaurants serve thinly sliced beef, tangy soups, and shrimp crêpes. Though the area is absolutely fascinating to explore, it's really not advisable to walk through Uptown late at night. Map B3

9 Lincoln Square

Beer, bratwursts, and grainy rye breads are order of the day in this bustling German enclave, where a 96-ft (29-m) outdoor mural depicts a rural German village. The hub of activity is a relatively small strip of Lincoln Avenue, between Lawrence and Western Avenues. The area maintains Old World charm with its German shops, delicatessens, bakeries, and an old-fashioned apothecary. Map B3

10 Bridgeport

First called Hardscrabble, this South Side neighborhood is one of the city's oldest, being settled in the 1830s by Irish laborers who came to help build the Illinois-Michigan Canal. Bridgeport still has a mostly Irish population, and has bred five Chicago mayors, including Richard J. Daley (see p35) and his son, Richard M. Daley. The area centerpiece is US Cellular Field (formerly Comiskey Park), home ground of the Chicago White Sox (see p51). Map B5

Next Pages **Mexican Mural, Pilsen**

Left **Mi Barrio Taqueria, Pilsen** Right **Mural, Lincoln Square**

⁑⁒10 Ethnic Neighborhoods

1 Pilsen
Named after a city in the former Czech Republic, whose immigrants settled here in the mid-1800s, this neighborhood now claims the Midwest's largest Mexican community. It's anchored by the Mexican Fine Arts Center Museum *(see p38)* and animated by street vendors, mariachi music, and Mexican restaurants. Vibrant outdoor murals and mosaics portray Mexican culture and history. *Map B5*

2 Avondale
In the early 20th century, menial jobs at Avondale's local factories and brickyards attracted many hard-working Polish immigrants. Today, the area also has many Hispanics, but it's still known as Little Warsaw because Chicago holds the largest concentration of Poles outside the Polish capital. Milwaukee Avenue and the neighboring streets also abound with bakeries, bookstores, delis, and a Polish Museum. *Map B4*

Building detail in Chinatown

3 Devon Avenue
Chicagoans who crave cheap, authentic Indian food head north to Devon Avenue in Rogers Park. Nineteenth-century English settlers named it after Devonshire, but since the 1960s, it's been a thriving Indian community, mingled with Russian, Greek, Syrian, and Jewish enclaves. From colorful saris to Indian videos to savory curried meats, it's almost like being in Delhi. *Map B3*

4 Andersonville
Amid a mix of Middle-Eastern and Asian cultures, the late-19th-century Swedish heritage here still makes its presence felt with billowing yellow and blue flags, Swedish bakeries and shops, and the Swedish-American Museum *(see p38)*. Adding to the minority mix is an increasing gay population – more laid-back than Boys Town *(see p85)* – evident in a number of trendy, gay-owned restaurants. *Map B3*

5 Little Italy, Taylor Street
The rich smells of garlic, basil, and baking bread waft from restaurants that line one of Chicago's oldest southern Italian neighborhoods. Though the streets have fewer Italians than when immigrants arrived in the late 19th century, you'll still see Italians chatting on street corners and toting groceries from Italian markets. *Map G6*

6 Heart of Italy
Northern Italians settled here in the 1920s, and some Chicagoans argue that this west side neighborhood is actually

Chicago Air Show

festive marine parade that culminates with fireworks over the lake. For the best views try Monroe Harbor at the lakefront. ☏ 312-744-3315 • Late Jul/early Aug

8 Chicago Air & Water Show
This massive display of military power features historic aircraft flybys, a staged amphibious attack, and precision flying teams. Prime beachfront viewing spots are from Oak Street to Montrose Beach. ☏ 312-744-3315 • Mid-Aug

9 Chicago Jazz Festival
Just as the Blues Fest ushers in summer, the smaller Jazz Fest caps it. Music fans are drawn to Grant Park for free concerts by a range of jazz greats like Branford Marsalis and Roy Hargrove.
☏ Map L6 • 312-744-3315 • Late Aug/early Sep (inc. Labor Day weekend)

10 Magnificent Mile Holiday Lights Festival
Merchants mark the start of the holiday season by lighting the shops, lampposts, and trees along Michigan Avenue. The parade and fireworks above the Chicago River on the Saturday night before Thanksgiving warrant braving the inevitable chill.
☏ Map L2 • Mid Nov–end Dec

Top 10 Sports Teams & Events

1 Chicago Cubs
Despite the Cubbies' losing streak, their baseball games are often sell-outs (see p85).

2 Chicago White Sox
The White Sox are renowned for their top-quality baseball. ☏ 312-674-1000 • www. whitesox.com • Apr–Sep

3 Chicago Bears
A football team generating rabid fans and tailgate picnics on Soldier Field (see p12) game days. ☏ 1-847-295-6600 • www. chicago bears.com. • Sep–Dec

4 Chicago Bulls
Their basketball just hasn't been the same since superstar Michael Jordan left. ☏ 312-455-4000 • www.bulls.com • Oct–Apr

5 Chicago Blackhawks
NHL ice hockey team sharing the United Center (see p13) with the Bulls. ☏ 312-455-7000 • www. chicagoblackhawks.com • Oct–Apr

6 Arlington Park
Thoroughbreds race just north of Chicago. ☏ 1-847-385-7500 • www.arlingtonpark.com • May–Sep

7 Chicago Fire
Many local Latino soccer fans support the Fire. ☏ 1-888-657-3473 • www.chicago-fire. com • Apr–Oct

8 Chicago Wolves
AHL's Wolves have a better playoff record than NHL's Blackhawks. ☏ 1-800-843-9658 • www. chicagowolves.com • Oct–May

9 Chicago Marathon
27,000 entrants run through the city. ☏ 312-904-9800 • www. chicagomarathon.com • Oct

10 Chicago Triathlon
Over 6,000 run, bike, and swim in this one-dayer. ☏ www. chicagotriathlon.com • Aug

For information on Chicago Events **See p109**

Left **Taste of Chicago** Center **Venetian Night** Right **Chicago Gospel Music Festival**

🔟 Festivals & Events

1 Chicago Blues Festival
The raucous weekend-long Blues Festival kicks off summer in Chicago. An estimated 750,000 listeners converge on Grant Park for the world's largest free blues event. The main stage line-up spans traditional bluesmen like Honey Boy Edwards, jazz inter-preters such as Mose Allison, and blues-inflected popsters like Bonnie Raitt. Smaller side stages offer a more intimate audience experience. ◈ Map L6 • 312-744-3315 • Late May–early Jun

2 Chicago Summer Neighborhood Festivals
Chicago is a city of neighborhoods with upwards of 100 neighbor-hood festivals to prove it. Virtually every summer weekend features an event or three ranging from the gay-oriented North Halsted Market Days to the ethnic Korean Street Festival.
◈ 312-744-3315 • May–Sep

Neighborhood festival in Chinatown

3 Chicago Gospel Music Festival
For three days Grant Park resounds with stirring choirs and impassioned soloists. Headliners have included R&B-star-turned-Memphis-preacher, Al Green. ◈ Map L6 • 312-744-3315 • Early Jun

4 Old Town Art Fair
This 50-year-old fair installs 250 artist booths along Old Town's historic and leafy lanes. The artwork is supplemented by food vendors, kids' entertainment, and garden tours. ◈ 1763 N. Park Ave. • Off Map • 312-337-1938
• www.oldtowntriangle.com • Jun • Adm.

5 Ravinia Festival
The summer home of the Chicago Symphony Orchestra, Ravinia stages concerts (classical, jazz, and pop) in suburban Highland Park. Sheltered seats are available but it's more fun to pack a picnic and join the crowds on the lawn. ◈ Off Map • 1-847-266-5100 • www.ravinia.org • Jun–Sep • Adm.

6 Taste of Chicago
Chicago's signature foods including deep dish pizza star during the nearly two-week long Taste. Musical entertainers, a carnival with rides, and cooking demonstrations entertain at the sprawling Grant Park event. ◈ Map L6 • 312-744-3315 • Late Jun–early Jul

7 Venetian Night
On this night, boat owners dress up their ships and form a

Unless otherwise indicated all festivals and events are free and have DA.

6 Second City

Since 1959, Chicago's famed Second City comedy troupe has launched such comic lights as John Belushi, Mike Myers, and Bill Murray. Actors improvize their lines in a series of skits connected by a current events theme on the cabaret-style main stage. Reservations are a must. ⊗ *1616 N. Wells St.* • *Map K2*
• *www.secondcity.com*

7 Court Theatre

This theater traces its roots to three Molière productions performed at the University of Chicago in 1955. The Court still mounts many classics, but it varies its seasons with musicals like *Guys and Dolls* and literary adaptations such as James Joyce's *The Dead.* ⊗ *5535 S. Ellis Ave.* • *Map E5* • *www.courttheatre.org*

8 Old Town School of Folk Music

Since the 1950s the Old Town School has brought world and homegrown folk music performers to Chicago. Its new home in Lincoln Square opened in 1998 with a concert by Joni Mitchell, though you're more likely to catch a women's ensemble from Mali and contemporary folkies such as Patty Larkin. ⊗ *4544 N. Lincoln Ave.* • *Map E3*
• *www.oldtownschool.org*

9 Lookingglass Theatre

In 1988, eight Northwestern University students founded Lookingglass, a bold company incorporating dance, circus arts, and live music in its original theatrical productions. Celebrity

Old Town School of Folk Music

membership (including *Friends* actor David Schwimmer) and Broadway bound, award-winning shows have furthered this company's stardom. ⊗ *821 N. Michigan Ave.* • *Map L2*
• *www.lookingglasstheatre.org*

10 Gene Siskel Film Center

Tiny by cineplex standards, the Gene Siskel Film Center screens films from the silent era onwards. Cineastes will rave about the cushy rocking chairs, excellent sightlines, and art gallery as well as foreign, independent and experimental films rarely shown elsewhere.
⊗ *164 N. State St.* • *Map K2*
• *www.siskelfilmcenter.com*

Left **Steppenwolf Theatre Co.** Right **Gene Siskel Film Center**

🔟 Arts Venues

1 Civic Opera House
This imposing Art Deco building is largely devoted to performances by the Lyric Opera. Each year (September through March), the company stages work by everyone from Wagner to Gilbert and Sullivan. Touring classical dance troops and musicals fill the off-season bill.
🌐 *20 N. Wacker Dr. • Map J4 • www.civicoperahouse.com*

2 Symphony Center
While visiting orchestras, lecturers, and jazz artists feature on its program, this center is first and foremost the home of the Chicago Symphony Orchestra directed by Daniel Barenboim. The complex holds a main stage, recital hall, and a bar-restaurant named Rhapsody *(see p75)*.
🌐 *220 S. Michigan Ave. • Map L6 • www.cso.org*

3 Steppenwolf Theatre Co.
Founded in 1974 in a church basement, Steppenwolf has gained acclaim based on the fame of its ensemble, which includes actor John Malkovich. Though the company has moved upscale to a specially built theater in Lincoln Park, it is still distinguished by raw emotion and edgy productions. 🌐 *1650 N. Halsted St. • Map E2 • www.steppenwolf.org*

4 Goodman Theatre
One of Chicago's leading theater companies, the Goodman frequently spins off

Court Theatre

productions to Broadway in New York and has earned a Tony award, the theater community's highest, for its efforts. Noted productions include dramas by Eugene O'Neill and August Wilson and an annual version of Charles Dickens' *A Christmas Carol*. 🌐 *170 N. Dearborn St. • Map K3 • www.goodman-theatre.org*

5 Chicago Shakespeare Theater
This Navy Pier venue presents a dynamic space for Shakespeare's repertory. The 510-seat courtyard design is inspired by the original layout in traditional playhouses of the Bard's day. Visiting non-Shakespeare productions take over after the company's September-to-April season.
🌐 *800 E. Grand Ave. • Map L3 • www.chicagoshakes.com*

brunch with seatings from 9:30am to noon is a must. ⓢ 329 N. Dearborn St. • Map K3 • 312-923-2000

6 Joe Segal's Jazz Showcase
Those reverent about jazz appreciate the cabaret-style Jazz Showcase. There's no smoking and a lot of shushing from the next table if you attempt to talk during a set. Consequently, musicians love the club, making this the spot to catch a date with Wynton Marsalis, Roy Hargrove, and other stars. As well as standard evening shows, the club offers Sunday matinees. ⓢ 59 W. Grand Ave. • Map K3 • 312-670-2473

7 Rosa's
Though off-the-beaten club path, the family-owned Rosa's is beloved citywide for its support of local artists such as blues harpist Sugar Blue and the genuine welcome by its owners, Tony Mangiullo and his mother Rosa. The latter sometimes cooks for the patrons of this simple tavern. ⓢ 3420 W. Armitage Ave. • Map E4 • 1-773-342-0452 • Closed Sun & Mon • www.rosaslounge.com

8 Green Dolphin St.
This slick Northside jazz club offers some of the city's best sightlines. Named for a jazz standard, Green Dolphin encompasses both a separate fine dining restaurant and an equally spacious showroom that also serves casual café fare. On the musical bill expect the sorts of ensembles that can audibly fill the space, such as big bands and Latin groups. ⓢ 2200 N. Ashland Ave. • Map D2 • 1-773-395-0066 • Closed Mon • www.jazzitup.com

9 Blue Chicago
Popular with tourists, Blue Chicago in River North operates

Buddy Guy's Legends

two clubs located two blocks apart. Seats at both venues are few and far between, so come early if you need one, or be prepared to dance. The admission charge covers both clubs, which encourages bar hopping. ⓢ 536 N. Clark St. & 736 N. Clark St. • Map K2 • 312-661-0100 • Closed Mon & Sun respectively

10 Andy's Jazz Club
With its musical programming that begins at lunchtime and continues into the evening, Andy's fills a void for those jazz fans who can't hold out for the late-night headliners. Prime perches are much sought after at the horseshoe-shaped bar in the no-fuss River North club. ⓢ 11 E. Hubbard St. • Map K3 • 312-642-6805

Left **Kingston Mines** Right **Green Mill Cocktail Lounge**

Blues & Jazz Joints

1 Kingston Mines
The largest of Chicago's blues joints, Kingston Mines packs its Lincoln Park locale with students, young professionals, and a broader spectrum of tourists. Two stages provide non-stop musical entertainment from 8pm to near 4am (5am on Saturdays). Acts range from homegrown house bands to national touring headliners. The kitchen serves up beer-sopping barbecue. ◈ *2548 N. Halsted St. • Map E2 • 1-773-477-4646*

2 Buddy Guy's Legends
A legend himself, bluesman Buddy Guy operates perhaps the best blues club in the city. The South Loop destination draws a mix of students, tourists, and local fans, particularly when Guy himself headlines. The place gets so packed that aisles are marked on the flooring and monitored by bouncers who make sure standing-room-only patrons keep them clear *(see p96)*.

3 B.L.U.E.S.
Among Chicago's many blues clubs, B.L.U.E.S feels the most like a Southern juke joint. Chalk it up to the narrow confines, loud sounds, and sweaty dancers. The club is across the street from the popular Kingston Mines, but it's a better choice for older, more musically versed blues fans. Better yet, why not stop into both! ◈ *2519 N. Halsted St. • Map E2 • 1-773-528-1012*

4 Green Mill Cocktail Lounge
A former Prohibition era speakeasy, Uptown's landmark Green Mill is a vintage treasure with a sweeping curved bar, vinyl booths, fading murals, and an authentic air of Chicago's gangster past. The city's premier jazz talents like Kurt Elling and Patricia Barber regularly play gigs here and Uptown Poetry Slam feature every sunday. It's out of the way but every cabbie knows how to get there. ◈ *4802 N. Broadway • Map E2 • 1-773-878-5552 • Limited DA*

5 House of Blues
Folk art and exotic architectural remnants festoon the funky House of Blues. The vast 1500-seat concert hall presents a variety of national touring acts from hard rock to hip hop in addition to blues. The Sunday gospel

Andy's Jazz Club

Unless otherwise stated all venues are open daily, charge admission, and have DA.

Sugar

gold-wrapped columns. Velvet chairs are free for lounging early on, but later they're reserved for big spenders. The dance floor fills up late, with DJs playing pop remixes. ◎ 537 N. Rush St. • Map L2 • 312-255-0022 • Closed Sun & Mon

7 Bin 36

This lofty space is a triple pleasure, with its high-end restaurant, casual café, and sociable wine bar. The large, zinc-topped oval bar is a lively setting for couples to share conversation and a cocktail, or for singles to mingle. "Wine flights" are a must-try, offering four half-glasses of different, but related, wines (see p83).

8 Le Bar

In the beautiful Sofitel Hotel (see p115), a fashionable, over-30, mixed crowd fills this lobby lounge after work, lingering until the wee hours. Black-clad servers dispense martinis with scrumptious flavors such as chocolate and raspberry. ◎ 20 E. Chestnut St. • Map K2 • 312-324- 4000 • Free

9 Sonotheque

This small, aluminum-clad nightclub forgoes dancing, and instead focuses on the pure enjoyment of the music. In fact, every visual aspect here serves to enhance the fantastic audio system: padded walls absorb sound, while the square-cut metal ceiling tiles diffuse it throughout the room. The sonic theme is further complemented by sleek steel and cool gray décor. ◎ 1444 W. Chicago Ave. • Map J2 • 312-226-7600 • Closed Mon • Free

10 Red Dog

Enter through the back doors in an alley parallel to North Avenue and head upstairs to Chicago's self-appointed "Supreme Funk Parlor". The high-energy, sardine-packed dance floor certainly lives up to its moniker. Monday is gay night, featuring Latin house music, while Friday night caters to hip-hop enthusiasts. The downstairs Border Line Tap bar is a perfect stop if you're early, or simply need a break from dancing. ◎ 1958 W. North Ave. • Map F4 • 1-773-278-5138 • Closed Tue, Thu, Fri & Sun

Left **Funky Buddha Lounge** Right **Bin 36**

Bars & Clubs

1 Sugar
This swank dessert bar transports you to a candy land, where light fixtures resemble honeycomb and bar stools look like hard candy. It's a novelty bar that gives perpetual dieters an excuse to indulge, if not in the sinful desserts offered, then at least in the luscious libations, such as ice wine, sweet martinis, or grappa. ⊗ 108 W. Kinzie St. • Map K3 • 312-822-9999 • Adm. Fri & Sat

2 Whiskey Sky
Nightlife goes sky-high at this intimate club on the 33rd floor of the W. Chicago Lakeshore hotel (see p117). Locals and guests mingle among '70s retro furnishings while soul and light house music provide the beat (though there's no dancing) to a backdrop of stunning views. ⊗ 644 N. Lake Shore Dr. • Map M3 • 312-255-4463 • Free

3 Zebra Lounge
An illegal speakeasy during Prohibition, this tiny piano bar has stood the test of time and

Zebra Lounge

competition, packing in loyal revelers nightly. Zebra prints dominate the décor, and martinis are the drink of choice. Singing along with the pianist to show tunes, torch songs, and oldies is expected (see p83).

4 Funky Buddha Lounge
This favorite is easily identified by the fat, happy Buddha statue outside. Inside, a mixed crowd of urban hipsters and young professionals sip everything from beer to bubbly in the low-ceilinged lounge. As the evening unfolds, the dance floor heats up with clubbers grooving to soul, salsa, hip-hop, R&B, house, rap, and reggae. ⊗ 728 W. Grand Ave. • Map K3 • 312-666-1695

5 Big Wig
You don't have to be a beauty school grad to let your hair down at this off-the-beaten-track dance club: in fact, helmet-style hair dryers serving as hanging lights are the only reference to the cute name. A varied crowd packs the neon-lit dancefloor, while local DJs spin techno, house, and hip-hop. Distortion Sundays feature punk and indie music, as well as cult and Kung Fu videos. ⊗ 1551 W. Division St. • Map J1 • 1-773-235-9100 • Closed Mon

6 Le Passage
Tucked along an alley and down a flight of stairs is the alluring Le Passage. The candlelit, wood-paneled room is divided by

Unless otherwise stated, bars and clubs are open daily, have a cover charge after 9/10pm, and have DA.

(see p52) qualifies as the best. Among them, Tiffin impresses with tender tandoori oven specialties and subtly spiced lentils. More upscale than most of its neighboring competitors, it generates a warm welcome via the enthusiasm of its staff. ⊗ 2536 W. Devon Ave. • Map B3 • 1-773-338-2143 • $$

Ann Sather

7 Ann Sather
Locals line up on Sunday mornings at the original Belmont Avenue Ann Sather for plates of oversized, sticky cinnamon rolls. But the Swedish diner makes a more ethnic appeal at lunch and dinner with *limpa* (Swedish rye bread), zesty duck with lingonberries, and hearty Swedish meatballs *(see p91)*.

8 The Berghoff
Holder of post-Prohibition liquor license number one, the Berghoff is a Chicago landmark, beloved for its 100-plus-year history as well as its traditional, robust German food. The Bavarian-styled dining rooms serve up generous portions of wiener schnitzel and sauerbraten as well as lighter fare for New World palates. The atmospheric standing-room-only tavern also sells sandwiches at lunch *(see p75)*.

9 Red Apple
In the heart of Polish Avondale, Red Apple offers budget priced, all-you-can-eat buffets, including dessert and coffee. The diner draws a cross-section of immigrants, artists, students, and the just plain thrifty for authentic dishes such as *pierogi*, borscht, goulash, and stuffed cabbage. ⊗ 3121 N. Milwaukee Ave. • Map B4 • 1-773-588-5781 • $

10 Fogo de Chao
The Sao Paulo owned Fogo de Chao specializes in the all-you-can-eat *churrascaria* tradition of Brazilian barbecue. At your table costumed "gauchos" will carve 15 different cuts of skewer-roasted meats, including filet, rumpsteak, leg of lamb, and pork loin. You can use a plate-side indicator to signal for more or "basta." A lavish salad bar begins every meal. ⊗ 661 N. LaSalle St. • Map K2 • 312-932-9330 • Closed Sat & Sun lunch • $$$$

Unless stated, all restaurants accept credit cards, recommend reservations, and are open for lunch and dinner.

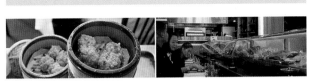

Left **Dim Sum at Phoenix** Right **Sushi Bar at Mirai**

Ethnic Eats

1 Arun's
Distinct from other Thai restaurants in the city, Arun's serves a gourmet version of the spice-and-vegetable driven Asian fare with high quality ingredients and careful presentation. Multicourse fixed-price menus change nightly, and dietary restrictions can be taken into consideration with advance notice. The quiet Thai art-trimmed rooms are conducive to conversation. ✪ *4156 N. Kedzie Ave.* • *Map B4* • *1-773-539-1909* • *Closed Mon, lunch* • *$$$$$*

2 Pasteur
Waitresses wearing pretty *cheongsams*, candles on the tables, and lush ferns on the room's periphery create a romantic setting for Vietnamese cuisine at Uptown favorite Pasteur. Best dishes include the assemble-your-own spring rolls. Continue with the aromatic *pho* soup and claypot chicken. ✪ *5525 N. Broadway* • *Map E2* • *1-773-878-1061* • *Lunch Thu–Sun* • *$$*

Tiffin

3 Phoenix
Superior Chinese dim sum, served with a panoramic view of downtown Chicago, garner out-the-door lines for this Chinatown gem. Dishes emerging from the kitchen are quickly snatched by waiting diners, leading many to ask for a table near it. ✪ *2131 S. Archer Ave.* • *Map A6* • *312-328-0848* • *$$*

4 Mirai Sushi
This hip, two-story eatery carves some of the city's best Japanese sushi. Options include the usual suspects such as tuna and salmon but for the most creative fare sit at the sushi bar, make a special request, and put yourself in the chef's hands. An upstairs lounge serves up sake martinis. ✪ *2020 W. Division St.* • *Map J1* • *1-773-862-8500* • *Closed lunch* • *$$$*

5 Ixcapuzalco
This off-the-beaten path, regional Mexican specialist is operated by a protégé of Rick Bayless of Frontera Grill fame *(see p41)*. Foodies head here for the outstanding *mole* sauces from Oaxaca, which change daily, and top fish, pork, chicken, or beef. ✪ *2919 N. Milwaukee Ave.* • *Map B4* • *1-773-486-7340* • *Closed Tue* • *$$$$*

6 Tiffin
Locals debate which Indian restaurant along the eatery-and-sari-shop-lined Devon Avenue

makes for a chic gourmet experience. The menu features seafood prepared with Asian flair and a light approach. ◈ *2039 W. North Ave.* • *Map F4* • *1-773-395-7100* • *Dinner only, closed Mon* • *$$$$*

7 Mia Francesca

The hearty, rustic fare of Rome and its surrounding regions distinguishes Mia Francesca from the Italian pack. Large portions and reasonable prices help draws legions of fans to this Wrigleyville rave. A former candy shop, the storefront eatery is casual but stylish with paper-topped tables and black-and-white photos of rural life on the walls. Lines form early and often *(see p91).*

8 Frontera Grill

Signature restaurant of chef Rick Bayless, Frontera Grill is credited with bringing authentic regional Mexican food – rather than Tex-Mex taco fare – stateside. Chili-roasted salsas and rich *moles* accompany grilled meats and delicious seafood. Since reservations are only available for parties of more than six, seats in the colorful, folk art-filled room go early as smaller groups try to avoid disappointment *(see p83).*

9 Pizzeria Uno

Uno's has been baking deep-dish pizza since 1943 – about as long as Chicagoans have debated whose pie is best. Its version comes several inches deep, filled with cheese and toppings of your choice, truly a meal in one slice. The smallish Victorian brownstone strains under demand, sending the overflow down the street to its spin-off Pizzeria Due. Uno's individual pizza served at lunchtime is a bargain. ◈ *29 E. Ohio St.* • *Map L3* • *312-321-1000* • *$*

Gibson's Steak House

10 Lou Mitchell's

A classic diner in the Loop where the waitresses call you "Honey" and the coffee is bottomless, Lou Mitchell's has been around since 1923. Its trek-worthy meal is breakfast, highlighted by double-yolk eggs and homemade hash browns served in a skillet. Tables turn quickly and the staff doles out free donuts and candy to those waiting on line with good cheer. ◈ *565 W. Jackson Blvd.* • *Map J4* • *312-939-3111* • *No credit cards* • *No dinner* • *$*

Unless stated, all restaurants accept credit cards, recommend reservations, and are open for lunch and dinner.

Hello Kitty! specialist, Sanrio. Across the hall from the Lego store, the Lego Construction Zone sets out Lego bricks for play. The fourth floor food court sells kid-favored foods like hot dogs and pizza. ◈ 520 N. Michigan Ave. • Map L2 • Open 10am–8pm Mon–Sat, 11am–7pm Sun

Navy Pier

7 Emerald City Theatre Company

In Chicago there's a theater company for every demographic and Emerald City is its troupe devoted to young audiences. Expect lively productions such as *Where the Wild Things Are* as well as holiday season shows in weekend-only midday matinees at Lincoln Park's Apollo Theater. ◈ 2540 N. Lincoln Ave. • Map E3 • Open Mon 10am–6pm, Tue–Fri 10am–8pm, Sat10am–9pm & Sun 11am–7pm • www.emeraldcitytheatre.com • Adm.

8 Museum Of Science & Industry

Though this museum dazzles kids and adults alike with its submarine ship and replica coal mine, it's The Idea Factory that's designed just for Junior. With the pulling of gears and shifting of knobs, kids experiment through play with balance, construction, magnetism, and more. A current-fed waterway encourages boat building. Arrive early on weekends or expect to have to wait for access *(see pp16–19)*.

9 Wrigley Field

A baseball lover's park, Wrigley is a small and intimate stadium that's far less intimidating for children than many larger stadia *(see p85)*. A ticket to anywhere in the grandstand allows you to walk around and get

to the rooftop terrace with its great views: the outfield stands can get rowdy, but a neighboring family section bans the beer that fuels the "bleacher bums."

10 The Café at American Girl Place

Vendor of dolls with educational aims, American Girl Place feeds its fantasy world, literally, in a café where dolls are welcome in clip-to-the-table chairs. Lunch leans to simple crowd-pleasers like tomato soup, while dinner supplies standards like chicken potpie. In between, the imaginative tea proffers chocolate pudding in a flowerpot or heart-shaped sandwiches. Reservations recommended *(see p82)*.

Left **Endo Exo, Armitage Avenue** Center **State Street Store** Right **Bloomingdale's Home Store**

Shopping Destinations

1 State Street
A slew of chain stores line this legendary street *(see p70)*, but it's the two old-time department stores that make it unique. Marshall Field's *(see p74)*, on this strip since 1907, has merchandise to satisfy every wealthy woman's needs. At Carson Pirie Scott & Co., the prices are lower, but the variety is still extensive *(see p74)*.

2 Magnificent Mile
Some 450 stores make this stretch of North Michigan Avenue one of the world's retail meccas. Besides sophisticated designer boutiques, there are malls (each with high-end department stores); and big-name chain and flagship stores *(see pp26–7)*.

3 Oak Street
If you have to ask how much it costs, you should probably plan on just window-shopping along

Prairie Avenue Bookshop

this stretch of Chicago's upper-crust Gold Coast. Boutiques here sell designer wear, accessories, and shoes fit for a Paris runway – and include some shops exclusive to Chicago such as Tessuti (menswear) and Designs by Ming (custom clothing design). ⊗ *Borders: N. Michigan Ave. & Rush St. • Map L1*

4 Jeweler's Row
This small strip in the Loop boasts a large number of jewelers that sell everything from discount diamonds to top-of-the-range gems. The Jeweler's Center at the beautiful 1912 Mallers Building *(see p74)* packs about 50 wholesale and retail jewelers and appraisers into 13 floors.

5 Bucktown Neighborhood
Once a hot-spot for starving artists, Bucktown and adjacent Wicker Park are now gentrified locales brimming with vintage clothes stores, edgy music shops, high-style designer boutiques, and antiques importers. ⊗ *Borders: Fullerton Ave. to North Ave. & Kennedy Expressway to Western Ave. • Map B4*

6 Broadway Antique Market
An old-time movie palace marquee indicates the 1939 building that houses this market. With 85 dealers stocking artwork, jewelry, clothing, and more in styles such as Arts and Crafts, Art Deco, and Victorian, you're sure to find something that pleases. ⊗ *6130 N. Broadway • Map E2 • Open 11am–7pm, Mon–Sat, 11am–6pm Sun • DA*

7 Prairie Avenue Bookshop

It's fitting that a city known for its architecture has one of the best architectural bookstores in the world. Besides carrying a range of 17,000 new and 7,000 out-of-print titles, the store is also appointed with furniture designed by Frank Lloyd Wright, Mies van der Rohe, and Le Corbusier (see p74).

8 Chicago Architecture Foundation Shop

Located in the historic Santa Fe Center (see p72), this shop is part of the CAF's ArchiCenter, which also puts on exhibitions and runs city tours. Browse the shop for architecture and design-related books; art-glass panels and lamps in Frank Lloyd Wright designs; desk gadgets; and desirable kitchen gizmos. ✪ 224 S. Michigan Ave. • Map L6 • Open 9:30am–6:30pm Mon–Sat, 9:30am–6pm Sun • DA

9 Bloomingdale's Home & Furniture Store

This store's lovingly restored 1913 Moorish-style building is an attraction in its own right. Inside there's a sleek, four-level atrium with home decor departments that sell everything from high-thread-count bedding to chic cookware and top-quality furniture. ✪ 600 N. Wabash Ave. • Map K3 • Opening times vary • DA

10 Armitage Avenue

This tree-lined street in Lincoln Park (see p85) is a favorite for those who are seeking out-of-the-ordinary clothing, home decor, bath and body products – and don't mind spending more to get it. Have patience finding a parking spot on weekends; once you're in, just shop-hop from one adorable boutique to the next.

Top 10 Souvenirs

1 Frango Mints
Marshall Field's (see p74) doesn't make these meltaway mint chocolates anymore, but it still sells them by the box-full.

2 Blues & Jazz CDs
CDs by Chicago music legends are on sale at the Water Tower Visitor Information Center (see p109).

3 Cows on Parade
Mini versions of the highly decorated cows from 1999s "Cows on Parade" display are sold at the ArchiCenter store.

4 Art poster
See the real thing, then buy a copy at the extensive Art Institute gift shop (see p8).

5 Michael Jordan Jersey
No longer a Bull, but he's still a star. Buy Jordan's merchandise at United Center's (see p13) Fandemonium store.

6 Cubs baseball cap
Head to the Tribune Tower (see p27) gift shop for caps of the Major League team owned by the Chicago Tribune.

7 Art glass
Get a little Prairie style with a replica Frank Lloyd Wright art-glass panel from the Chicago Architecture Foundation store.

8 Chicago mugs
The Chicago Historical Society (see p86) sells mugs depicting the faces of famous local residents like Al Capone.

9 Sue skeleton
Sue, the world's largest T. rex skeleton is far less menacing in mini model form from the Field Museum (see p14).

10 Chicago snowglobe
Recall Chicago winters with a city skyline snowglobe from Accent Chicago in the Water Tower Place mall (see p26).

For more on shopping in Chicago See pp74, 82, 88, 102, 113.

Left **Scene from** *The Relic*, **set at the Field Museum** Right **Andy Garcia in** *Hero*, **Drake Hotel**

10 Film Locations

1 Daley Center & Plaza

Daley Plaza *(see p73)* with its famed Picasso sculpture was the setting for a sensational chase scene in cult movie classic *The Blues Brothers* (1980). Stars John Belushi and Dan Aykroyd, playing ex-criminal brothers, dramatically crash their car through the center's plate-glass windows, specially installed for the filming, as the authorities hopelessly attempt to stop them.

2 James R. Thompson Center

In *Running Scared* (1986) Billy Crystal and Gregory Hines are Chicago police pals planning early retirement, but first they must thwart a drug kingpin and stay alive. The final chase scene takes place in the Thompson Center *(see p37)* where the two swap wisecracks while swinging on ropes through the airy atrium, shooting out glass elevators, and ultimately triumphing.

3 The Art Institute of Chicago

The consummate high school comedy *Ferris Bueller's Day Off* (1986) stars Matthew Broderick,

While You Were Sleeping **at the Sedgewick El Station**

Exterior of State of Illinois Center as featured in *Running Scared*

who skips school and takes his girlfriend (Mia Sara) and best friend (Paul Ruck) on an action-packed Chicago day. At the Art Institute, Broderick and Sara kiss in front of a window designed by Chagall, while Ruck stares intensely at *A Sunday on La Grande Jatte –1884 (see p8)*.

4 Union Station

Elliott Ness (Kevin Costner) brings down Chicago gangster Al Capone (Robert DeNiro) in the true story *The Untouchables* (1987). In one unforgettable scene, a shoot-out on a Union Station staircase causes a mother to lose her grip on her baby carriage, which bounces in slow motion down the stairs, saved at the last moment by Ness's partner.
🕾 *210 S. Canal St.* • *Map J5*

5 Drake Hotel

In feel-good film *Hero* (1992) John Bubber (Andy Garcia) dupes the public into thinking he's a hero. Feeling guilty, he resolves to jump off a window ledge at The Drake (see p115). Reality interrupted the filming when guests arrived for a party at the hotel. Director Stephen Frears protested so violently, he almost got arrested.

A scene from *Chain Reaction* on Michigan Avenue Bridge

The Hilton Chicago
6 Wrongly accused and convicted of murder, Dr. Richard Kimble (Harrison Ford) dodges the authorities led by Tommy Lee Jones to prove his innocence in *The Fugitive* (1993). He winds up in a pulse-pounding chase through this grand hotel (see p116) onto its roof, down its elevator shaft, and into the hotel's laundry room.

Sedgwick El Station
7 The El tracks are an apt symbol of hard-working Chicago, and they feature significantly in the romantic comedy *While You Were Sleeping* (1995). Sandra Bullock plays an El station clerk who falls in love with a handsome commuter. He tumbles off the platform, Bullock saves his life, and comedy and romance ensue. ◈ Map J1–2

Field Museum
8 Scare-fest *The Relic* (1997) starred Penelope Ann Miller and Tom Sizemore as researchers trying to stop a murderous monster before it killed again. Many interior scenes were shot on replica sets but were near-perfect matches to the real museum (see pp14–15).

Michigan Avenue Bridge
9 *Chain Reaction* (1996) sees Keanu Reeves as a science student at the University of Chicago (see pp28–9) who is framed for murder. In a nail-biting chase scene, he tries to escape by running up the Michigan Avenue Bridge (see p27) as it's raised.

Wrigley Building
10 In *Road to Perdition* (2002) Tom Hanks is Michael Sullivan, an Irish gangster living in 1930s Chicago. After his wife and young son are murdered, he flees town with his older son. In seeking a safe refuge, they enter a hotel, the exterior of which is the beautiful Wrigley Building (see p27). However, the interior scenes were actually filmed at The Hilton Chicago.

Left **Blues Festival, Grant Park** Right **Gold Coast seen from Oak Street Beach**

🔟 Parks & Beaches

1 Millennium & Grant parks
As well as a center for world-class art, music, architecture and landscape design, the 24-acre (10-ha) Millennium Park offers winter ice skating, interactive public art, al fresco dining and free classical music concerts. Together with the adjoining 19th century Grant Park, which hosts many of the city's varied and vibrant festivals (see pp50–51), it constitutes one of the finest, user-friendly green spaces in Chicago (see p71).

2 Lincoln Park
The greenway Lincoln Park stretches from North Avenue up to Hollywood Avenue, a recreational apron between lakefront and housing. In Chicago's infancy, the southern portion of the park was a cemetery for Civil War dead, later ex-humed and interred else-where to make way for the park. Now it's the North Side's counterpart to Grant Park. Popular attractions such as Lincoln Park Zoo (see pp24–5), the Lincoln Park Conservatory (see p86), and Peggy Notebaert Nature Museum (see p85) supplement the beaches, harbors, playing fields, and bike paths. ⊗ Map F3

The Republic, Jackson Park

3 North Avenue Beach
Chicago's most populist beach, North Avenue Beach

attracts a broad range of urban-dwellers. Its lively ocean-liner-shaped bathhouse (which includes umbrella rentals, shower rooms, snack vendors, and a rooftop restaurant) makes it particularly family friendly. Rows of beach volleyball courts draw teams often made up of impromptu players, and a seasonal outdoor gym welcomes day use (see p86).

4 Oak Street Beach
At the foot of the tony Gold Coast shopping lane, Oak Street Beach reflects its environs. Though just next to North Avenue Beach, you won't see many children here. With its emphasis on flesh and flash, Oak Street is usually filled with toned bodies and tiny bikinis. Still, the crescent-shaped strand is the closest beach to the Magnificent Mile (see pp26–7) and makes a great place to stop and dip your toes after some serious shopping. ⊗ Map L1

5 Jackson Park
Laid out by the famed land-scape designer Frederick Law Olmsted for the 1893 World's Columbian Exposition, Jackson Park, along with its Museum of Science & Industry (see pp16–19), is among the few developments still remaining from that World's Fair. The Southside park includes a Japanese garden with waterfalls,

All city beaches have lifeguards on patrol 9am–9:30pm, Memorial Day–Labor Day.

Bathhouse, North Avenue Beach

colorful lanterns, and a bird sanctuary on an island in a peaceful lagoon. ◈ Map F6

6 Burnham Park

Designed by and named for city planner Daniel Burnham, Burnham Park is the city's green lawn rolling south from Museum Campus (see p92) to Hyde Park. Like Lincoln and Grant parks, it is charted by the lakefront bike path, but unlike its northern counterparts Burnham Park's section isn't overrun, making this south-leg journey far more enjoyable. Along the way you'll find basketball courts and beaches. The return trip north provides city skyline panoramas. ◈ Map C6

7 Montrose Beach

Stretching nearly to Wilson Avenue, Montrose is spacious where downtown beaches are jammed. Convenient for swimmers, this North Side spot includes a changing house and shower facilities. The vast playing fields wedged between the sand and Lake Shore Drive are the domain of Hispanic soccer clubs: on weekends their numbers draw Latin food and balloon vendors. Look for kayak rentals that launch here in summer. ◈ Map C3

8 Foster Beach

Near the northern end of the lakefront bike path, Foster Beach proves a timely spot to cool off. There's a snack bar, and the nearby picnic tables and grills draw family crowds. A beachside basketball court hosts lively free-for-all games to which only the talented should apply. ◈ Map B3

9 Olive Park

A pocket-sized park just beside Navy Pier (see pp20–21), Olive Park makes great strolling grounds. Jutting into Lake Michigan just off Ohio Street, it provides skyline views similar to Navy Pier's though without the tourist mobs. Quiet and out of the way, this is one of the city's most romantic parks. ◈ Map M2

10 Washington Square

Opposite the historic Newberry Library, Washington Square is a prime plot of Gold Coast for resting tired feet and gazing at the handsome 1892 building. The park's ample benches tend to draw bookish sorts and picnicking office workers at lunchtime. ◈ Map K2

For information on bike rental See p108

Left **Chicago Botanic Garden** Center **Church window, Historic Pullman District** Right **IIT**

Sights off the Beaten Track

1 Garfield Park Conservatory

Beneath glass-domed roofs, flora from around the world thrives in spacious greenhouses. Information panels give the low-down as you stroll through the conservatory's six indoor areas that include a Children's Garden and the Sweet House (containing plants such as cacao, sugar cane, etc). ◈ *300 N. Central Park Ave.* • *Map B5* • *312-746-5100* • *El station: Conservatory-Central Park Dr. (green line)* • *Open 9am–5pm daily, Thu 9am–7pm* • *Free* • *DA*

2 Chicago Botanic Garden

About 25 miles (40 km) north of Chicago, this attraction comprises 385 acres (155 ha) of natural habitats and beautifully landscaped gardens. Some of the most popular are the romantic Rose Garden, the tranquil island-based Japanese Garden, and the charming English Walled Garden. ◈ *1000 Lake Cook Rd. Glencoe* • *1-847-835-5440* • *Map A1* • *Metra station: Glencoe* • *Open 8am–sunset daily* • *Free* • *DA*

Grosse Point Lighthouse, Evanston

3 Historic Pullman District

This industrial town was conceived in the 1880s by railroad magnate George Pullman for his workers. The planned utopia had apartments, shops, a hospital, and a hotel, but failed after a strike in 1894, when a decrease in wages made rents unaffordable. ◈ *Map C6* • *Metra Station: Pullman/111th St.* • *Visitor Center: 11141 S. Cottage Grove Ave., open 11am–3pm Tue–Sun* • *1-773-785-8901* • *DA*

4 Illinois Institute of Technology (IIT)

In 1940, Ludwig Mies van der Rohe planned the campus of this new university. He also designed around 20 of the buildings, which demonstrate his design philosophies. Stop by the on-campus visitor center for information and self-guided tours. ◈ *3201 S. State St. (Visitor Center)* • *Map C5* • *312-567-3000* • *El station: 35th-Bronzeville-IIT (green line)* • *Free* • *DA*

5 Sheridan Road

This lakefront road's low speed limit is perfect for gawping at the palatial, architecturally diverse homes that line it as you drive north to Evanston and beyond. Art buffs might like to stop at the Martin D'Arcy Gallery at Loyola University, which specializes in art from Medieval to Baroque times. ◈ *From Rogers Park to Lake Bluff* • *Map B3* • *Martin D'Arcy Gallery, 6525 N. Sheridan Rd., 1-773-508-2679, open noon–4pm Mon–Fri, Free, DA*

6 Bronzeville

A bronze memorial at Martin Luther King, Jr. Drive and 35th Street honors the journey many African-Americans made to this neighborhood as they fled the oppression of the South in the early 20th century. Nearby, sidewalk plaques celebrate local luminaries. Chicago's answer to Harlem offers jazz and blues in its clubs, graceful mansions aplenty, and lots of fine soul food. ⊗ Map C5 • El station: 35th-Bronzeville-IIT (green line)

7 Baha'i Temple

This exquisite white structure is one of eight temples of the Baha'i faith worldwide. Its nine doors symbolize how people can come to God from any direction. At night, spotlights enhance its ethereal beauty. ⊗ 100 Linden Ave, Wilmette • Map A1 • El station: Linden Ave (purple line) • Open 10am–8pm daily (Oct–May to 5pm) • 1-847-853-2300 • Free • DA

8 Historic Long Grove

Thanks to strict regulations, the 19th-century heritage of this quaint town 30 miles (48 km) northwest of Chicago has been preserved. The candy-filled Long Grove Confectionery store is a local institution. Annual events include the popular Chocolate Festival. ⊗ Off Map • At Route 83 & Old Route 53 • Visitor Center: 1-847-634-0888 • Open Mon–Sat 10am–5pm, 11am–5pm Sun

9 Brookfield Zoo

Over 5,900 animals live together in themed, naturalistic environments at this popular zoo. Zones include Tropic World, where thunderstorms occur regularly (you stay dry) and Habitat Africa, whose new Forest exhibit has shy okapi and a re-created African village. In Be A Bird House, see what kind of bird you'd be on a

Baha'i Temple

machine that measures your flapping ability. ⊗ 3300 Golf Rd, Brookfield • Map A5 • Metra station: Hollywood • Open 10am–5pm daily (to 6pm Sat & Sun) • 1-708-485-2200 • Adm. (2 and under, free) • DA

10 Evanston

Just north of Chicago, this dynamic suburb brims with acclaimed restaurants, galleries, and independent shops. Northwestern University's Mary and Leigh Block Museum of Art and Sculpture Garden is well worth a visit, as is the historic Grosse Point Lighthouse and Maritime Museum adjacent to the campus. ⊗ Map B2 • Visitors Bureau 1-847-328-1500 • El station: Davis

AROUND TOWN

CHICAGO'S TOP 10

Left **Harold Washington Library Center** Right **Elevated train, The Loop**

The Loop

NAMED AFTER THE RING OF ELEVATED TRAIN TRACKS *that encircle it, this is downtown Chicago's core, and the city's financial and governmental hub. Abuzz with laptop-toting business folk during the week, the Loop is transformed on weekends when a veritable shopping frenzy erupts along its famous State Street. Those thirsty for culture also come flocking to view the area's many architecturally significant buildings and notable public art. A recent infusion of corporate dollars has given the Loop a real boost: the resulting restoration of old theaters and the promotion of the theater district has lured in more visitors, and the many great bars and restaurants that have sprung up mean that the area now offers a burgeoning nightlife.*

Lion, Art Institute of Chicago

Sights

1. Art Institute of Chicago
2. Sears Tower
3. Chicago Cultural Center
4. The El
5. Harold Washington Library Center
6. Chicago Board of Trade
7. State Street
8. State of Illinois Center
9. The Rookery
10. Millennium & Grant parks

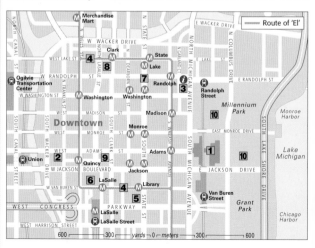

1 The Art Institute of Chicago

This extraordinary collection of exhibits spans over 4,000 years of international art, much of it donated by wealthy Chicago collectors (see pp8–11).

2 Sears Tower

An architectural superlative, the tower offers breathtaking bird's-eye views from its 103rd floor Skydeck, where you'll find yourself standing on top of 76,000 tons of steel (see pp12–13).

3 Chicago Cultural Center

Built in 1897 as the city's first main library, this magnificent Beaux Arts building was described at the time as the "people's palace." In 1991, the library moved out, allowing several galleries, performance spaces and a visitor information center to move in. Guided tours offer a historical overview of the building, which occupies an entire block and features one of the world's largest domes, designed by L. C. Tiffany, and rooms modeled after the Doge's Palace in Venice and the Acropolis in Athens. ✆ 77 E Washington St. • Map L4 • 312-744-6650 • Open 10am–7pm Mon–Thu, 10am–6pm Fri, 10am–5pm Sat • Tours 1:15pm Wed, Fri & Sat • Free • DA

4 The El

Originally called the Union Loop, this system of elevated trains came about after the 1871 Great Chicago Fire (see p34) when the city was rebuilt with such unexpected success that, within 20 years, its streets could no longer handle the influx of people, streetcars, and horses filling them. Today, three lines ring the business district – the

Tiffany Dome, Chicago Cultural Center

Orange, Purple, and Brown lines – with three others connecting it to destinations farther afield (see p56).

5 Harold Washington Library Center

Named after former city Mayor Harold Washington, Chicago's first Afro-American mayor (see p35), this is the largest public library building in the country. Its collections, which include a superlative Blues Archive and a vast children's library, fill an incredible 70 miles (110 km) of shelving. Architects Hammond, Beeby, and Babka incorporated architectural elements of several Chicago landmarks, such as The Rookery (see p70) and The Art Institute (see pp8–9) in the building's design: don't miss the ninth-floor Winter Garden atrium, which soars two stories to a spectacular glass dome. ✆ 400 S. State St. • Map K5 • Open 9am–7pm Mon–Thu, 9am–5pm Fri & Sat, 1–5pm Sun • Free • DA

Sears Tower

Borrow piano sheet music at the Harold Washington Library and tickle the ivories in one of the six free-to-use practice rooms.

59

6 Chicago Board of Trade

The Chicago Board of Trade (CBOT) was founded in 1848 to create a central marketplace in the fast-developing city, and moved to its current 45-story home in 1930. Designed by Holabird and Root, this landmark building is a stunning example of Art Deco. Capping the majestic limestone building is a huge statue of Ceres, the Roman goddess of grain and harvest. A glittering 23-story glass-and-steel addition designed by Helmut Jahn was completed in 1980. ◈ *141 W. Jackson Blvd.* • *Map K4* • *Closed to the public until further notice*

7 State Street

This "great street" got its nickname from the 1922 hit song *Chicago*. Although it didn't always live up to this catchy moniker, it has won back many fans since its multi-million-dollar face-lift in 1996. It now sports replica Art Deco lampposts and subway entrances, and was listed on the National Register of Historic Places in 1998. This dynamic stretch has it all: shopping, history, education, architecture, theater, and dining. The atmosphere is especially merry during the run up to Christmas, when the Thanksgiving parade brings Santa to town, and department stores like Marshall Field's *(see p74)* fill their windows with elaborate and imaginative decorations. ◈ *From Wacker Dr. to Congress Parkway* • *Map K4*

The Loop's Sculpture

Setting a trend for public artwork Downtown, Pablo Picasso's untitled sculpture, simply known as "the Picasso," was donated to Chicago in 1967. The Loop's street corners now accommodate more than 100 sculptures, mosaics, and murals by both established and upcoming artists. A free guide to the open-air artworks – the *Loop Sculpture Guide* – is available from the Chicago Cultural Center *(see p68)*.

8 James R. Thompson Center

Also known as the State of Illinois Center, this striking 17-story, steel and granite structure shimmers with 24,600 curved glass panels. Helmut Jahn designed the controversial 1985 building to be a democratic fusion of government offices and public spaces, such as shops, restaurants, and art galleries. The soaring skylit atrium is sliced by internal glass elevator shafts and contains unusual, see-through escalators. Outside, the plaza features the intriguing 1984 sculpture *Monument with Standing Beast* by Jean Dubuffet. ◈ *100 W. Randolph St.* • *Map K4* • *Atrium, shops, & food court open to public: 8:30am–6pm Mon–Fri* • *Free* • *DA*

9 The Rookery

This 11-story building, with its rusticated red granite base, was the country's largest office building and a precursor to modern skyscrapers when it was completed in 1888 by Burnham and Root *(see p37)*. Its stunning skylit lobby was

Buckingham Fountain, Grant Park

State of Illinois Center

redesigned in 1907 by Frank Lloyd Wright *(see pp30–31)*, who added a grand staircase and hanging light fixtures, both of which carry his signature circle-in-square motif. The building's unusual name refers to the rooks that once roosted at the site. ✆ *209 S. LaSalle St.* • *Map K4* • *Open 9am–5pm Mon–Fri* • *Free* • *no DA*

10 Millennium & Grant parks
The modern Millennium Park *(see p62)* is Chicago's superb new adaptation of its "front yard". The park is home to a dynamic Frank Gehry-designed music pavilion and pedestrian bridge, and a vast sculpture by British artist Anish Kapoor. It also boasts lush gardens, restaurants, a winter ice rink, peristyle, and an interactive fountain by Spanish artist Jaume Plensa. The adjoining Grant Park *(see p62)* hosts many summer festivals including the Taste of Chicago *(see p50)*. It is also home to Museum Campus *(see p92)*, the Art Institute of Chicago *(see pp8–11)*, and the ornate 1927 Buckingham Fountain. ✆ *Map L6 & L4* • *Open daily* • *Free* • *DA*

A Day in The Loop

Morning

🕐 Start early with breakfast at the charming Atwood Café in the lobby of the historic **Hotel Burnham** *(see p116)*, with its beautifully reconstructed interior. Then stroll a block west to Daley Plaza to see the giant unnamed **Picasso sculpture**, stopping off at the Hot Tix booth at 78 W Randolph Street, to get half-price, same-day tickets to a Loop theater performance. Continue along Michigan Avenue, past the **Chicago Cultural Center** *(see p68)*, and south to **The Art Institute of Chicago**. A whirlwind tour of the highlights *(see pp10–11)*, all conveniently located on the upper level, can be done in a couple of hours, though you may want to come back for a second helping.

Afternoon

Either have lunch in The Art Institute's outdoor café or head west along **State Street** to eat at **Marshall Field's** *(see p74)* legendary seventh-floor Walnut Room, a Chicago fixture since 1907. Then burn off the calories by shopping your way around the vast store and along the famous street that it's situated on. For pre-theater dining, try the sophisticated **Rhapsody** *(see p75)*, convenient for the **Symphony Center** *(see p48)* Or, on weekdays, try the all-you-can-eat buffet at **Trattoria No. 10** *(see p75)*.

Evening

After the show, hop a quick cab ride to stylish **Nine** *(see p75)* for a cocktail or some dancing late into the night in the slick second-floor Ghost Bar.

Left **Chicago Theater** Center **Fisher Building** Right **One North LaSalle**

Architectural Sites

1 Monadnock Building
At 16 stories, this Holabird and Roche designed building (1891) is one of the world's tallest all-masonry high-rises. Inside, there's a magnificent wrought-iron staircase *(see p36)*. ◈ *53 W. Jackson Blvd.* • *Map K4*

2 Marquette Building
Holabird and Roche also built this 1895 Chicago School structure with a steel skeleton and decorative ornamentation. ◈ *140 S. Dearborn St.* • *Map K4*

3 Reliance Building
Daniel H. Burnham's stunning glass-and-white-glazed-terracotta building (1895) is now the Hotel Burnham *(see p116)*.

4 Fisher Building
Another Chicago School edifice with a steel structure, this 1896 neo-Gothic building is also by Daniel H. Burnham. Aquatic motifs on the façade honor the building's first owner, L. G. Fisher. ◈ *343 S. Dearborn St.* • *Map K5*

5 Carson Pirie Scott Building
Eye-catching cast-iron swirls on part of the exterior of this store (1899 & 1903) express architect Louis H. Sullivan's love of elaborate detail *(see p74)*.

6 Santa Fe Center
Daniel H. Burnham designed this elegant high-rise in 1904: its carved building signs are from

Chicago's days as a railroad hub. The ground level houses the Chicago Architecture Foundation *(see p59)*.

7 Chicago Theater
The red marquee of this Beaux Arts-style theater is a symbol of Chicago. Built in 1921, today it is a performance venue. ◈ *175 N. State St.* • *Map K4*

8 One North LaSalle
This 1930-built, 49-story building was Chicago's tallest for 35 years, and is one of the city's best surviving examples of Art Deco architecture. ◈ *Map K4*

9 Inland Steel Building
One of the first skyscrapers to be built (in 1957) on steel, not concrete, pilings. It predated the John Hancock building *(see p12)* in using external supports. ◈ *30 W. Monroe St.* • *Map K4*

10 Federal Center
Flanked by Ludwig Mies van der Rohe's federal buildings, this plaza (1959–74) contains Alexander Calder's striking statue *Flamingo* (1974). ◈ *219 S. Dearborn St.* • *Map K4*

For more on Skyscrapers See p36–7

'2

Left **Civic Opera Building** Center **Old St. Patrick's Church** Right **Palmer House Hilton**

🔟 Best of the Rest

1 Loop Theater District
A sidewalk plaque at Randolph and State Streets denotes Chicago's Theater District, a cluster of old and new theaters. ⊗ *Map K4*

2 Civic Opera House
This 1929 structure was inspired by Paris's Opera Garnier. Inside, there are gleaming marble floors, crystal chandeliers, and a grand staircase *(see p48)*.

3 Symphony Center
At the heart of this center is Orchestra Hall (1904), the home of the Chicago Symphony Orchestra. A major 1997 extension added offices and the Rhapsody restaurant *(see p48)*.

4 Old St. Patrick's Church
Chicago's oldest church (1856) is crowned by two towers – one Romanesque, one Byzantine – symbolizing East and West. ⊗ *700 W. Adams St. • Map J4*

5 Fine Arts Building
This historic landmark was designed by Solon S. Beman and completed in 1885. It was used as a carriage showroom by the Studebaker Company and today houses a gallery and two movie theaters. ⊗ *410 S. Michigan Ave. • Map L5*

6 Chicago Temple
A Gothic-inspired structure that was designed by Holabird and Roche in 1923. Under the majestic spire is a 35-seat chapel. ⊗ *77 W. Washington St. • Map J4*

7 Federal Reserve Bank
This impressive structure is one of 12 regional Reserve banks. When it was first built in 1922, it had the largest bank vaults ever constructed. ⊗ *230 S. LaSalle St. • Map K4*

8 Palmer House Hilton
The first Palmer House was destroyed in the Great Chicago Fire *(see p34)*. The current grand hotel is the third version and is lavishly decorated with frescos, Tiffany light fixtures, and marble floors *(see p116)*.

9 Daley Plaza
The location of the county court headquarters, Daley Plaza is best known for its giant steel unnamed Picasso sculpture (1967), donated by the artist. It was mocked when unveiled, but is now a city icon. ⊗ *Map K4*

10 *Four Seasons*
Chagall's glittering 70-ft (21-m) long, rectangular slab (1974) is covered in thousands of tiles that depict the cycle of the seasons. ⊗ *First National Plaza, at Dearborn and Monroe • Map K4*

Left **Artwork for sale in Gallery 37** Center **Clock at Marshall Field's** Right **Carson Pirie Scott & Co.**

🔟 Shops

1 Marshall Field's
Chicago's oldest and best-known department store is most famous for its elaborate Christmas displays, dazzling Tiffany dome, and iconic clock. Nearly 100 years after opening, this flagship store continues to offer top styles for home and body *(see p59)*.
⊗ *111 N. State St. • Map K2 • DA*

2 Carson Pirie Scott & Co.
You'll find some fantastic budget-friendly buys as well as a dreamy shoe department in this ornate, historic, 12-story department store *(see p72)*.
⊗ *1 S. State St. • Map K4 • DA*

3 Sears on State
After 18 years away, a hipper Sears returned to State Street in 2000 offering five levels of everything from tools to toddler outfits.
⊗ *2 N. State St. • Map K2 • DA*

4 Prairie Avenue Bookshop
This wonderful bookstore is the world's largest that is dedicated to architecture and related fields. It's a staple for architecture students, but also a fascinating browse for anyone. ⊗ *418 S. Wabash Ave. • Map K4 • Closed Sun • DA*

5 Jeweler's Center
On the strip commonly known as "Jeweler's Row" this one-stop-shop is a friendly place to source gold, pearls, watches, diamonds, and gems at relatively low prices. ⊗ *5 S. Wabash Ave. • Map K4 • Closed Sun • DA*

6 Nordstrom Rack
High style on sale at a fraction of the original prices lure bargain hunters to this charming little sister of the upscale and pricey Nordstrom.
⊗ *24 N. State St. • Map K4*

7 Poster Plus
This enormous store opposite The Art Institute of Chicago *(see pp8–11)* sells contemporary, vintage, and collectors' posters, as well as artsy gifts. ⊗ *200 S. Michigan Ave.• Map L6 • DA*

8 Gallery 37 Store
Teenage artists involved in an arts training program create the incredible paintings, sculptures, and other artwork sold here. All proceeds from sales are returned to the program.
⊗ *66 E. Randolph St. • Map L4 • Closed Sun • DA*

9 Old Navy
This regional flagship store offers the ultimate Old Navy shopping experience, with two floors of discount jeans and T-shirts, and other casual comfort clothes at bargain prices.
⊗ *35 N. State St. • Map K2 • DA*

10 Iwan Ries Tobacco
A smoker's paradise since 1897, this store now sells around 100 cigar brands, 15,000 pipes, and countless smoking accessories. It also contains a small tobacco museum. ⊗ *19 S. Wabash Ave. • Map K2 • Closed Sun • DA*

Store opening hours are at least from 10–5pm (Chains & Department Stores to 8pm) Mon–Sat & 11–6pm Sun.

Price Categories

Price categories include a three-course meal for one, a glass of house wine, tax, and a 15–20% tip.	**$** under $20
	$$ $20–$30
	$$$ $30–$45
	$$$$ $45–$60
	$$$$$ over $60

Russian Tea Time

 Places to Eat & Drink

1 Nine
This hip restaurant specializes in steaks and seafood. There's also a champagne bar and the Ghost Bar for drinks and dancing. ◈ 440 W. Randolph St. • Map J4 • 312-575-9900 • Closed Sat lunch & all day Sun • $$$$

2 Everest
The restaurant on the top floor of the Chicago Stock Exchange has dazzling views and to-die-for chocolate soufflé. ◈ 440 S. LaSalle St. • Map K5 • 312-663-8920 • Closed lunch, Sun & Mon • $$$$$

3 Rhapsody
A perfect choice for modern American food (like the signature onion-crusted sturgeon) before or after a concert. ◈ Symphony Center, 65 E. Adams St. • Map L4 • 312-786-9911 • Closed Sat lunch & Sun • $$$$

4 The Berghoff
Founded in 1898, this German institution is adored for such hearty food as wiener schnitzel and sauerbraten. ◈ 17 W. Adams St. • Map J4 • 312-427-3170 • Closed Sun • $$$

5 Trattoria No. 10
Ravioli and risotto are the specialties here. A $12 buffet (plus $6 drink minimum) is available Monday through Friday evenings. ◈ 10 N. Dearborn St. • Map K3 • 312-984-1718 • Closed Sat lunch & Sun • $$$$

6 Catch 35
This sophisticated seafood restaurant has live piano jazz in the evenings. Don't miss the lime pie.
◈ 35 W. Wacker Dr. • Map K3 • 312-346-3500 • Closed lunch Sat & Sun • $$$$

7 Ada's Famous Deli
Walk right in for generous portions of deli favorites such as matzo ball soup and stuffed cabbage. ◈ 14 S. Wabash Ave. • Map K4 • 312-214-4282 • $

8 Atwood Café
Expect top-notch hotel dining, where creative American cuisine leans toward comfort food. ◈ Hotel Burnham, 1 W. Washington St. • Map J4 • 312-368-1900 • $$$$

9 Italian Village Restaurants
Choose between upscale Vivere, The Village with its extensive menu, or mid-priced La Cantina – all under the same roof. ◈ 71 W. Monroe St. • Map K4 • 312-332-4040 (Vivere), 312-332-7005 (The Village & La Cantina) • Days closed vary • $$$–$$$$ • No DA

10 Russian Tea Time
A spirited taste of Russia, where the vodka flows freely and the beef stroganoff is a crowd-pleaser. ◈ 77 E. Adams St. • Map L4 • 312-360-0000 • $$$$

Unless otherwise stated, all restaurants recommend reservations, accept credit cards, have DA, and are open for lunch and dinner.

Left **Merchandise Mart** Center **Tiffany vases** Right **Carl Hammer Gallery, River North Gallery District**

Near North

HISTORY, CULTURE, AND COMMERCE *collide on Chicago's densely-packed Near North side. This area is a pleasure to explore on foot, whether motivated by a penchant for shopping or an appreciation of fine art and architecture. The city's toniest shopping boulevard – the Magnificent Mile, a.k.a. the Mag Mile – bridges the posh 19th-century mansions of the lakeside Gold Coast (which has its own clutch of upscale boutiques) and the former industrial warehouses of River North, now mostly converted into art galleries. In addition to these, two local art museums prove that "exhibitionism" in Chicago isn't just about the Art Institute (see pp10–11). But ultimately, it's the Magnificent Mile on a Saturday that says more about Midwestern vitality and giddy American consumerism than any other Chicago experience.*

Observation Deck, John Hancock Center

🔟 Sights

1. Magnificent Mile
2. John Hancock Center
3. Merchandise Mart
4. Museum of Contemporary Art
5. River North Gallery District
6. Gold Coast Area
7. Historic Water Tower & Pumping Station
8. Tribune Tower
9. Fourth Presbyterian Church
10. Hershey's Chicago

Previous Pages **James R. Thompson Center**

Magnificent Mile

Magnificent Mile
1 Whether you're a shopper or not, this store-lined strip warrants a visit if only to get a feel for the commercial pulse that seems to keep Chicago humming *(see pp26–7)*.

John Hancock Center
2 Skidmore, Owings & Merrill designed this 1970 landmark using the signature X's on the facade as cross-braces to help the 1,100-ft (335-m) building withstand the winds coming off Lake Michigan. An alternative to soaking up the view from the 94th-floor observatory is drinking it in from the Signature Room restaurant and lounge on the floors directly above. Many say you get a better view from here than from the South Side's Sears Tower – and the lines are usually shorter too. ⓢ *875 N. Michigan Ave. • Map L2 • Observatory open 9am–11pm daily, Adm., DA • Signature Room open 8am–6pm Mon–Fri, 8am–1pm Sat, DA*

Merchandise Mart
3 This massive two-square-block edifice houses Chicago's premier interior design trade showrooms. When completed in 1930, the four million-sq-ft (390,000-sq-m) building was the largest in the world. Today, it is second only to the Pentagon in size, and is still the world's largest commercial building. A 90-minute guided tour includes a visit to several showrooms. ⓢ *300 N. Wells St. • Map K3 • Free • DA • Tours 1pm Mon & Fri, call 312-527-7762*

Museum of Contemporary Art
4 One of the country's largest collections of international contemporary art, the MCA displays over 6,000 objects, from painting and sculpture to photography and video installations. Trendy Spago chef Wolfgang Puck runs the airy café, which draws both museum-goers and Mag Mile shoppers alike. In summer, the terraced sculpture garden enhances the MCA experience, while the front lawn often plays host to displays of performance art. ⓢ *220 E. Chicago Ave. • Map L2 • Open Tue–Sun 10am–5pm (to 8pm Tue) • Adm. (free on Tue evenings) • DA*

Sculpture, Museum of Contemporary Art

River North Gallery District
5 Said to be the most concentrated art hub in the US outside of Manhattan, this district is jammed with great galleries. Most are to be found in the handsome, 19th-century, converted brick warehouses found along either side of the El brown line. Huron and Superior Streets are particularly worth a visit. ⓢ *Bounded by Merchandise Mart (south), Chicago Ave. (north), Orleans Ave. (west), Dearborn St. (east) • Map K3 • River North Association 312-645-1047 • www.rivernorthassociation.com*

Stained glass, Fourth Presbyterian Church

castellated Gothic-Revival Water Tower, modeled after a medieval castle, was once called a "monstrosity" by critic Oscar Wilde. It now houses the City Gallery (specializing in photography), and the fountain and chairs outside make it a focal point for downtown street life. The Water Pumping station across the street still functions, and also houses a visitor center and the Lookingglass Theater, co-founded by *Friends* star David Schwimmer. ◈ *Map K2 • Water Pumping Station & Tower 163 E. Pearson St., Visitor Center open 7:30am–7pm daily, 312-744-2400 • City Gallery open 10am–6:30pm Mon–Sat, 10am–5pm Sun, Free, DA*

6 Gold Coast Area

Chicago boasts many upscale neighborhoods, but none more historic and prestigious than the Gold Coast. Railroad, retail, and lumber tycoons built this elegant district in the decades following the Great Fire of 1871 *(see p34)*, and its leafy streets are lined with 19th-century mansions interspersed with early 20th-century apartment buildings. There are no less than 300 designated historic landmarks in the Astor Street District alone, including buildings by Stanford White (such as 20 E. Burton Place), and Charnley House, designed by Louis Sullivan (assisted at the time by Frank Lloyd Wright). (1365 N. Astor Street). ◈ *Map K1*

Historic Water Tower

7 Historic Water Tower & Pumping Station

When the Great Fire of 1871 swept north, only the 1869 Water Tower and Pumping Station escaped ruin. Built by William W. Botington, the

8 Tribune Tower

Topped by flying buttresses, this Gothic-style building was completed in 1925. Its faux historic design had won a competition organized by Colonel Robert McCormick, publisher of the *Chicago Tribune*, the newspaper whose offices still occupy the building. Look closely at the facade, which is embedded with over 120 stones collected by correspondents from famed sights. There's a rock hailing from each of the 50 states, as well as fragments from international monuments such as Greece's Parthenon, India's Taj Mahal, and The Great Wall of China. ◈ *435 N Michigan Ave • Map L3 • Tours by appointment*

9 Fourth Presbyterian Church

The first Fourth Presbyterian church, dedicated in 1871, celebrated its first sermon just hours before it was incinerated in the Great Fire. Rebuilt in 1914 when

Magnificent Mile was the little-used Pine Street, today's church offers a peaceful respite from the now highly commercial boulevard. Designed by Ralph Adams Cram, one of the architects behind New York's Cathedral of St. John the Divine, it's not surprising that this church boasts a cathedral-like interior, with an impressive stained-glass west window. A tranquil courtyard is often the place for classical concerts in summer. § 126 E. Chestnut St. • Map K2 • Open 9am–6pm daily • Free • DA

10 Hershey's Chicago

When candy-manufacturer Milton Hershey visited the city of Chicago in 1893, he purchased the equipment that he would use to revolutionize the chocolate industry. With mass production he was able to lower the cost of manufacturing milk chocolate, once a luxury item, making it affordable to all. Today, the Hershey Foods Corporation is the largest North American producer of chocolate and non-chocolate confectionary. Hershey's Chicago, a new themed store on Magnificent Mile, stocks all the well-known brands such as *Hershey's*, *Reese's*, and *Kit Kat*, as well as the latest products and goods unique to the Chicago store. Sugar-free versions of the most popular products are also available. A hit with children is the store's interactive "bake shoppe" where visitors can customize cookies, cupcakes, and brownies. § 822 N Michigan Ave • Map L2

Store sign for Hershey's Chicago

A Day in the Near North

Morning

Line up early with the locals for a fortifying stack at The Original Pancake House (22 E. Bellevue Pl.). Afterward, stroll south on Rush Street to Oak Street. Take a left and walk the most exclusive shopping block in the city, where you can pop into stores such as Barneys New York. Once you hit Michigan Avenue, it's a short jaunt to the **John Hancock Center** (see p79) and its sky-high views. Back on terra firma, cross the street to the **Historic Water Tower** for a close-up look at a piece of Chicago's history. Lovers of modern art should cross Michigan again and head to the **Museum of Contemporary Art** (see p79) with its spacious galleries and sculpture garden.

Afternoon

Everyone will get what they want for lunch at Foodlife, a gourmet food court on the second level of the mall in **Water Tower Place** (see p26). You can shop the seven floors of Chicago's first ever vertical mall, and then shop some more – and sightsee – along the **Magnificent Mile** (see pp26–7). If you've worked up an appetite, stroll over to the **Drake Hotel** (see p115) for high tea, which serves until 5pm.

Evening

Alternatively, NoMI in the **Park Hyatt Chicago** (see p115) serves stylish contemporary fare (reservations needed), as befits the neighborhood. Or just join the smart set over cocktails at the Bar at the **Peninsula Chicago** (see p115).

Left **American Girl Place** Right **Paper Source**

Shopping

1 Ultimo
Oak Street's toniest designer boutique, Ultimo carries a range of cutting-edge European and American lines for women as well as men. ◎ *114 E. Oak St.* • *Map L1*

2 Barneys New York
This branch of the Big Apple's downtown department store draws together the latest cosmetics, shoes, jewelry, accessories, and men's and women's apparel in a minimalist, open-plan, tri-level space. ◎ *25 E. Oak St.* • *Map L1*

3 Bloomingdale's
An outpost of New York's hometown department store that features in-store designer boutiques and a well-stocked shoe department. ◎ *900 N. Michigan Ave.* • *Map L2*

4 Ikram
Launched by a former Ultimo buyer, Ikram specializes in high-end women's fashion sold at top dollar. Chic wares and lines change seasonally, but shop assistance is uniformly personal. ◎ *873 N. Rush St.* • *Map L2*

5 Polo/Ralph Lauren
This massive four-story shop so thoroughly transforms itself from a store to a swell den devoted to Lauren's to-the-manor-born lifestyle – note the horse and hound paintings throughout – that it warrants a visit from even the less well-heeled among us. ◎ *750 N. Michigan Ave.* • *Map L2*

6 American Girl Place
Parents accompanying girls age four to 12 make a beeline to this store, the only retail outlet of the popular American Girl line of dolls. A theater and café *(see p57)* supplement three floors devoted to dolls, books, and accessories. ◎ *111 E. Chicago Ave.* • *312-943-9400* • *Map L2*

7 Anthropologie
Women's apparel with a bohemian bent and housewares gathered from around the world sell briskly at this loft-like store. ◎ *1120 N. State St.* • *Map K2*

8 P.O.S.H.
Recalling the days of elegant steamships and grand hotels, this store uses old-fashioned suitcases and steamer trunks to lovingly display vintage china and silverware engraved with hotel and ship logos. ◎ *613 N. State St.* • *Map K2*

9 Paper Source
This arty River North shop is part art supply store, part stationer. The creative selection of cards and small gifts includes handmade stationery, cloth-covered sketchbooks, and novel desktop accessories. ◎ *232 W. Chicago Ave.* • *Map J2*

10 Fly By Nite Gallery
Amid the River North fine art galleries, Fly By Nite sells Art Nouveau and Art Deco decorative arts, including malachite jewelry, art-glass lamps and vases, and collectible pottery. ◎ *714 N. Wells St.* • *Map K2*

> *Most Near North shops are open 10am–7pm Mon–Sat & 11am–6pm Sun and have DA.*

Price Categories

Price categories include a three-course meal for one, a glass of house wine, tax, and a 15–20% tip.

$	under $20
$$	$20–$30
$$$	$30–$45
$$$$	$45–$60
$$$$$	over $60

Frontera Grill

🔟 Places to Eat & Drink

1 Frontera Grill
Chef Rick Bayless' regional Mexican cuisine warrants the two-margarita waits that inevitably face diners here. ◎ 445 N. Clark St. • Map K2 • 312-661-1434 • Closed Sun & Mon • Reservations only for groups of 5+ • $$

2 Keefer's
A steakhouse that goes beyond the men's club stereotype, also serving French specials and ample fish selections. ◎ 20 W. Kinzie St. • Map K3 • 312-467-9525 • Closed Sun & lunch Sat • $$$

3 Bin 36
A wine bar of warehouse proportions, Bin 36 engenders an infectious enthusiasm for wine and food. The many small dishes encourage sampling. ◎ 333 N. Dearborn St. • Map K3 • 312-755-9463 • $$$

4 RL
An in-store steakhouse and power-eatery, furnished in upper crust style by the Ralph Lauren Home shop while elegantly attired hostesses sport Polo. ◎ 115 E. Chicago Ave. • Map L2 • 312-475-1100 • $$$$

5 Pierrot Gourmet
Run by the elegant Peninsula hotel, this café serves inventive salads, open sandwiches and pastries. ◎ 108 E. Superior St. • Map L2 • 312- 573- 6749 • No reservations • $$

6 Coco Pazzo
In the gallery district Coco Pazzo prepares dramatic, earthy Italian cuisine in an impressive loft space. ◎ 300 W. Hubbard St. • Map K3 • 312-836-0900 • Closed Sat & Sun lunch • $$$$$

7 Spago
California chef Wolfgang Puck spins off a Chicago Spago to much acclaim. An open kitchen showcases the cooks preparing the east-west fusion fare. ◎ 520 N. Dearborn St. • Map K3 • 312-527-3700 • Closed Sat lunch and Sun • $$$$

8 Pump Room
A jazz trio, opulent decor, and a forward-leaning continental menu serve diners here. Celebrities love its famed "booth 1." ◎ 1301 N. State Pkwy. • Map K1 • 312-266-0360 • Closed Sat lunch • $$$$

9 Whiskey Bar & Grill
Run by Rande Gerber, husband of supermodel Cindy Crawford, this sophisticated, sleek bar attracts a trendy crowd. ◎ 1015 N. Rush St. • Map L2 • 312-475-0300

10 Zebra Lounge
A classic piano lounge, the Zebra is intimate, friendly, and decorated wall to wall in animal prints. It's a funky place to drink cocktails in the Gold Coast. ◎ 1220 N. State St. • Map K2 • 312-642-5140

> Unless otherwise stated, all restaurants recommend reservations, accept credit cards, have DA, and are open for lunch and dinner.

Left **Armitage/Halsted Shopping District** Right **Butterfly, Peggy Notebaert Nature Museum**

Northside

ENCOMPASSING PARTS OF OLD TOWN, *Lincoln Park, Lakeview, and Wrigleyville,* Chicago's Northside boasts upscale restaurants and chi-chi boutiques galore, as well as some of the city's best bars and one of its most progressive theater companies, the Steppenwolf (see p48). Older buildings have been transformed into beautiful condominiums, while stylish new apartments are springing up on empty lots. In season, nearby Wrigley Field fans bolster the lively Wrigleyville atmosphere by swarming the surrounding streets and bars – whether or not the Cubs win. The vibrant gay hub of "Boys Town" is also in this area, while running along Northside's eastern border is the incredible lakefront, with sand volleyball and a beach bar heating up as soon as the temperature allows.

Tiger, Lincoln Park Zoo

Sights

1. Lincoln Park Zoo
2. Wrigley Field
3. Peggy Notebaert Nature Musem
4. Boys Town
5. Armitage/Halsted Shopping District
6. Chicago Historical Society
7. Lincoln Park Conservatory
8. North Avenue Beach
9. Elks National Memorial Building
10. Francis Dewes Mansion

Lincoln Park Zoo

Who's watching who at this beloved city zoo, which attracts more than three million visitors annually (see pp24–5).

Wrigley Field

Built in 1914, this is the USA's oldest National League baseball park. Home team, the Chicago Cubs, haven't won a World Series championship since 1908 (before the field even existed), but that doesn't stop Northsiders from being behind them every step of the way. In season (March–September), spending an afternoon cheering on the "Cubbies" in this marvelous stadium, with its ivy-clad walls, is a quintessential Chicago experience.
§ 1060 W. Addison St. • Map D1 • 1-773-404-2827 • Box Office open 8am–6pm Mon–Fri, 9am–4pm Sat & Sun • Adm. • DA

Peggy Notebaert Nature Musem

This museum's sloping, beige exterior was inspired by the sand dunes that once occupied its site. Inside are a host of engrossing interactive exhibits, the highlight being the walk-through Butterfly Haven, a light-filled space, constantly aflutter. The outdoor grounds, with their native wild-

Wrigley Field

Boys Town

flowers and prairie grasses, are perfect for a peaceful walk or rest.
§ 2430 N. Cannon Dr. • Map F3 • 773-755-5100 • Open 9am–4:30pm Mon–Fri, 10am–5pm Sat & Sun • Adm. (free on Thu) • DA

Boys Town

Strolling down North Halsted Street, it's fairly evident you're in Chicago's gay neighborhood when you hit shops called Gay Mart, Cupid's Treasures, and a club named Manhole. Just 30 years ago, this area – officially East Lakeview – was pretty shabby, the bars were without signs, and parking was a cinch. But now buzzing Boys Town is gay central – by day and by night.
§ N. Halsted St. (& much of Broadway) from Belmont Ave.–Grace St., & Clark St. from Belmont–Addison Aves. • Map E1–2

Armitage/Halsted Shopping District

This area of unique boutiques is a boon for fashionistas. Dozens of shops here sell everything from sophisticated evening wear to high-end accessories: many of the stores occupy renovated Victorian town homes, set along pretty tree-lined streets.
§ Armitage Ave. from Halsted St.–Racine Ave., & Halsted St. from Webster–Armitage Aves. • Map E4

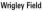
For more Chicago shopping **See pp58–9**

Lincoln Park Conservatory

6 Chicago Historical Society

Focusing on Illinois and Chicago history since settler days, this museum was established in 1856 and is the city's oldest cultural institution. One of the society's first donors bequeathed his collection of Lincoln memorabilia: the ex-president's deathbed is one of the items displayed. Visitors can also climb aboard the Pioneer locomotive, while events such as the World's Columbian Exposition and the Great Chicago Fire *(see p34)*, are brought to life by photographs, decorative arts, and other exhibits. There are also costumes belonging to famous local figures including sportsman Michael Jordan. ✪ *1601 N. Clark St. • Map K2 • Open 9:30am–4:30pm Mon–Sat, noon–5pm Sun • Adm. (free Mon) • DA*

Chicago Historical Society

7 Lincoln Park Conservatory

Take a free trip to the tropics at this spacious conservatory, just next to Lincoln Park Zoo. Opened in 1893, the glass structure is a year-round, 80° F (40° C) sanctuary from the Chicago's bustle, and offers a welcome respite from the city's long winters. Paths meander past lush palms, flourishing ferns, and exquisite 100-year-old orchids. Avoid the crowds by coming on a weekday when, unless a seasonal show is taking place, it's a quiet space, with the sound of trickling water as background music. ✪ *2400 N. Stockton Dr. • Map F3 • Open 9am–5pm daily • Free • DA*

8 North Avenue Beach

When summer finally graces Chicago with its presence, locals of all ages and nationalities converge on this short, but inviting stretch of beach. Running along its edge is the lakefront path, where cyclists, in-line skaters, runners, and walkers stream by. An outdoor gym gives confident folks a place to strut their stuff, sand volleyball courts allow the energetic to let off steam, and the rooftop bar of the steamship-shaped beach house is perfect for downing a cool drink while lazily watching the activity below. ✪ *Lakeshore Dr. & North Ave. • Map F4 • Open dawn to dusk • Lifeguards on duty from Memorial Day–Labor Day.*

For more on Chicago parks and beaches **See pp62–3**

9 Elks National Memorial Building

The Benevolent and Protective Order of Elks, an American fraternity (founded in 1868 and still going strong), built this magnificent structure in 1926 to honor its World War I veterans. It's since been re-dedicated to pay homage to World War II, Korean and Vietnam war veterans. Two larger-than-life elk statues flank the wide entrance steps, while inside, every inch is richly decorated. The 100-ft (30-m) marble rotunda, murals depicting the Sermon on the Mount, intricate windows, and allegorical bronze sculptures are awe-inspiring. ◎ *2750 N. Lakeview Ave. • Map E2 • Open 9am–5pm Mon–Fri; mid-Apr–mid-Nov also open 10am–5pm Sat & Sun • Free • DA*

10 Francis Dewes Mansion

Nostalgic German immigrant Francis Dewes, a self-made millionaire, commissioned this elaborate home in 1896. Built in the eclectic Gründerzeit style – a German counterpart to Beaux Arts – its entrance steps, stone statues, and ornate carved curlicues certainly stand out from the neat rows of adjacent brick apartment buildings. Interior highlights include mosaic floors, a fountain, and wrought-iron chandeliers. ◎ *503 W. Wrightwood Ave. • Map E3 • 773-216-5700 • Call for opening times*

Francis Dewes Mansion

Exploring Northside

Morning

Fuel up for the day at one of Lincoln Park's favorite breakfast joints, **Frances'** (2552 N. Clark St.), where they serve a wonderfully fluffy French toast. Afterwards, stroll east down Wrightwood Avenue, and you'll pass the ornate **Francis Dewes Mansion**. Keep walking until you come to the **Lincoln Park Zoo** (see pp24–5), where you can take a ride on the wild side on the African Safari motion simulator, complete with 3D visuals. Then see all the animals in person, before breaking for lunch with a view at **Café Brauer**, built in 1908 by Prairie School architect Dwight Perkins.

Afternoon

During warm weather, head to the lakefront along Fullerton Avenue where you can stroll, rent bikes, sunbathe, or even brave the ever-chilly Lake Michigan waters. In colder months, catch a bus (nos. 22 or 151) and immerse yourself in the exhibits at the **Chicago Historical Society**, or take a five-minute cab ride to **Armitage/Halsted Shopping District** (see p85) for some classy retail therapy.

Evening

This part of town has an abundance of good eateries: hop the El four stops or cab it to try **Mia Francesca's** (see p41), a lively Italian trattoria where the pasta dishes are big enough for two, and there's an excellent wine list. Still going strong? Round off your day with a visit to **Kingston Mines** (see p46) – just a short cab-ride away – to hear some of best blues that the city has to offer.

Left **Barker & Meowsky** Right **Cynthia Rowley**

TOP 10 Shops

1 Isabella Fine Lingerie
This charming boutique has something silky, soft, and sexy for women whose sizes range from barely there to 44JJ. You'll also find teddies, bustiers, pajamas, and nightgowns.
◊ *1101 W. Webster St. • Map E3*

2 Cynthia Rowley
Internationally acclaimed clothing designer Cynthia Rowley grew up in Chicago, so it's fitting that one of her upscale boutiques is here. Her collection of dresses, accessories, and separates is trendy and feminine.
◊ *808 W. Armitage Ave. • Map E4*

3 Lori's Designer Shoes
Devoted shoe hounds flock to this Lincoln Park store for its hot styles at discounted prices. The floors and walls are stacked high with boxes for handy self-serve try-on access. ◊ *824 W. Armitage Ave. • Map E4*

4 Lincoln Antique Mall
This huge mall is chock-full of treasures from vintage purses to kitschy dinnerware and Art Deco glass. Prices are typically negotiable. ◊ *3141 N. Lincoln Ave. • Map E3*

5 Unabridged Bookstore
Known for its large gay and lesbian section, this Boys Town *(see p85)* bookstore also stocks books of all types, particularly kids' and Spanish language books. ◊ *3521 N. Broadway. • Map E2*

6 Hubba-Hubba
Women appreciate this boutique for its romantic and flirty vintage fashions and jewelry. It also sells new items with a retro feel. ◊ *3309 N. Clark St. • Map F4*

7 Silver Moon
At this shop, vintage and antique clothing, jewelry, and furniture are meticulously labeled with price, size, and decade.
◊ *3337 N. Halsted St. • Map E2*
• Closed Mon & Tue

8 Barker & Meowsky
Four-legged friends are the focus at this store. From ceramic dog bowls to catnip-filled toys, rhinestone-studded collars to cookie-shaped dog biscuits, this store is a pet's best friend.
◊ *1003 W. Armitage Ave. • Map E4*

9 Uncle Fun
This toy store is especially fun for grownups who yearn to feel like a kid. You'll find retro items like Mr. T coloring books, silly accessories like oversized sunglasses, and gag gifts like the tried-and-true whoopie cushion.
◊ *1338 W. Belmont Ave. • Map E2*

10 Nuada
Named after an ancient legendary fish god, this Celtic-inspired boutique brings contemporary design to ancient crafts. High style wares include home accessories, jewelry, fine art, gifts and knitwear. ◊ *1022 W. Armitage Ave. • Map E4*

→ *Most of these stores are open from at least 11am–7pm Mon–Sat & noon–5pm Sun, unless otherwise stated, and they all have DA.*

78

Left **Kit Kat Lounge** Right **Bucks Saloon**

Gay & Lesbian Bars & Clubs

1 Circuit/Rehab
At Circuit, men often dance shirtless to grinding house music. In contrast, the Rehab lounge bar is a sophisticated chill-out spot. § 3641 N. Halsted St. • Map E2 • Circuit: open Thu–Sun, Adm.

2 The Closet
This dance club attracts a mostly lesbian crowd, but gay men and straight couples also groove to R&B, rap, dance, and diva videos. § 3325 N. Broadway • Map E2

3 Roscoe's Tavern
A young, preppy set packs this neighborhood bar for its antique décor, cozy fireplace, poppy dance tunes, pool table, and, in summer, backyard beer garden. § 3356 N. Halsted St. • Map E2

4 Sidetrack
Find some of the best cruising at this vast, four-room bar with more than two dozen video monitors that highlight a different theme (like show tunes or 1980s music) every night. § 3349 N. Halsted St. • Map E2

5 Spin
One of Boys Town's most diverse clubs: gay, lesbian, bi, and straight crowds mingle at this dance club and lounge. § 800 W. Belmont Ave. • Map E2

6 Kit Kat Lounge & Supper Club
Martinis come in 52 flavors at this swanky spot, where female impersonators divert attention from significant others with their lip-synching talent. § 3700 N. Halsted St. • Map E2 • Closed Mon

7 Berlin
For 20 years, this edgy club has attracted every type from straight girls to drag queens. After midnight, the dance floor hits its peak, rocking with a stellar sound system and light show. § 954 W. Belmont Ave. • Map E2

8 Cocktail
This laid-back club is ideal for sipping must-try martinis, while Boys Town people-watching through wall-to-wall windows. § 3359 N. Halsted St. • Map E2

9 Gentry on Halsted
Piano players and singers perform nightly for appreciative and participative audiences at this cabaret club. § 3320 N. Halsted St. • Map E2

10 Bucks Saloon
A friendly, local bar (for boys and girls) where deer, elk, moose, and buck heads adorn the walls. The outdoor beer garden is wild in summer. § 3439 N. Halsted St. • Map E2

Unless otherwise stated, all bars and clubs do not charge admission, are open daily, and have DA. On weekends many stay open 'til 4am.

79

left **Guthrie's Tavern** right **Decorative Brickwork at Schubas Tavern & Harmony Grill**

TOP 10 Neighborhood Bars

1 Schubas Tavern & Harmony Grill
Twenty-somethings dress down for beer, live music, and a great restaurant that packs in crowds, especially on the patio during warm-weather weekends. ⊗ *3159 N. Southport Ave. • Map D1*

2 Four Farthings Tavern
This casual, family-owned bar is a perfect spot to kick back with one of 18 beers on tap, a single-malt whisky, or a glass of wine. ⊗ *2060 N. Cleveland Ave. • Map E3*

3 Bar Louie on the Park
With the chain's signature wrap-around bar and bright mosaics, this bar is a comfortable favorite for young professionals who appreciate the moderately priced drinks, plenty of tap beers, and huge sandwiches. ⊗ *1800 N. Lincoln Ave. • Map E3*

4 The Duke of Perth
This Scottish pub hits the mark, with nearly 90 varieties of single-malt whisky and plenty of Celtic paraphernalia and music. ⊗ *2913 N. Clark St. • Map F4*

5 Guthrie's Tavern
Amid chitchat and free pretzels, boisterous patrons play board games. Come early for the best choice. ⊗ *1300 W. Addison St. • Map D1*

6 John Barleycorn Memorial Pub
Disguised as a laundry during Prohibition, this cozy pub has been dispensing beer and spirits for over a hundred years. ⊗ *658 W. Belden Ave. • Map E3*

7 Red Lion Pub
British ex-pats hang here for a taste of home that fits the bill with plenty of pints from across the pond. Upstairs is an outdoor deck for warm-weather carousing. ⊗ *2446 N. Lincoln Ave. • Map E3*

8 Southport Lanes & Billiards
During the day, this is a laid-back bar: at night, a rowdy young crowd covets turns at the four hand-set bowling lanes. ⊗ *3325 N. Southport Ave. • Map D1*

9 Wrightwood Tap
The centrally positioned bar, promotes an open, *Cheers*-type feel, with conversation flowing among patrons. TVs typically air college sports, while dart boards provide participatory entertainment. ⊗ *1059 W. Wrightwood Ave. • Map E3*

10 The Tin Lizzie
A sports bar-and-dance club, Tin Lizzie is wall-to-wall with twenty- to thirtysomethings most weekend nights, when DJs spin a variety of tunes. ⊗ *2483 N. Clark St. • Map F4*

> Unless otherwise stated, all bars and clubs are open daily and have DA. At weekends many stay open until 2/3am.

Price Categories

Price categories include a three-course meal for one, a glass of house wine, tax, and a 15-20% tip.

$	under $20
$$	$20–$30
$$$	$30–$45
$$$$	$45–$60
$$$$$	over $60

North Pond

Restaurants

1 North Pond
This pond-side restaurant (a former skaters "warming house") serves up American gourmet cuisine. ◎ 2610 N. Cannon Dr. • Map F3 • 1-773-477-5845 • Closed Mon, lunch (except Jun, Jul, Aug, Sep, & Sun) • $$$$

2 Ambria
Tuxedoed staff set an elegant tone at this French special-occasion favorite. ◎ 2300 N. Lincoln Park West • Map F3 • 1-773-472-5959 • Closed lunch, Sun • $$$$$

3 Charlie Trotter's
Light French food is artfully designed by master chef Charlie Trotter at this internationally acclaimed restaurant. ◎ 816 W. Armitage Ave. • Map E4 • 1-773-248-6228 • Closed Mon & Sun, lunch • $$$$$

4 Geja's Café
The ultimate fondue in a romantic setting. Choose cheese or hot oil, or just opt for the divine chocolate dessert fondue. ◎ 340 W. Armitage Ave. • Map E4 • 1-773-281-9101 • Closed lunch • No DA • $$$

5 erwin
Chef Erwin Drechsler offers up a "melting-pot" cuisine, complemented by a superb wine list. Sunday brunch is a real treat. ◎ 2925 N. Halsted St. • Map E2 • 1-773-528-7200 • Closed Mon, lunch (except Sun) • $$

6 Tarasacas
Mexican food gets a fancy touch at this colorful restaurant. Nights get spirited as diners down huge margaritas. ◎ 2585 N. Clark St. • Map F4 • 1-773- 549-2595 • Closed lunch (except Sat & Sun) • $$

7 Robinson's No. 1 Ribs
The perfect, low-key spot for getting messy with thick, saucy barbecue ribs. A back patio opens during warm weather. ◎ 655 W. Armitage Ave. • Map E4 • 312-337-1399 • Closed Mon, Sat lunch • No DA • $$

8 Stanley's Kitchen & Tap
Comfort food, like macaroni cheese and apple pie, is the draw at this family-friendly spot. The all-you-can-eat brunch gets packed. ◎ 1970 N. Lincoln Ave. • Map E3 • 312-642-0007 • Closed Mon lunch • $$

9 Ann Sather
Known for its scrumptious breakfasts, this Swedish restaurant also serves lunch and dinner specialties such as meatballs. ◎ 929 W. Belmont Ave. • Map E2 • 1-773-348-2378 • $

10 Mia Francesca
The wait for the generous portions of flavorful pastas, seafood, and chicken at this lively eatery is definitely worth it. ◎ 3311 N. Clark St. • Map F4 • 1-773-281-3310 • Closed lunch • $$$

Unless otherwise stated, all restaurants recommend reservations, accept credit cards, have DA, and are open for lunch and dinner.

Left **Adler Planetarium** Right **Shedd Aquarium (left) & Field Museum (right), Museum Campus**

South Loop

JUST SOUTH OF THE *business-centric Loop, this sprawling area mixes ethnic enclaves such as Chinatown (founded in the 1870s by migrant transconti-nental railroad workers) with uppercrust addresses, built after the Great Chicago Fire of 1871 (see p34). The region has many Chicago "must-sees," but the jewel in the crown is undisputedly the impressive Museum Campus: here, the Field Museum, John G. Shedd Aquarium, and Adler Planetarium celebrate the wonders of the earth, sea, and sky respectively, collectively drawing over four million visitors each year. The highway that once separated the Field from its neighbors has been replaced by an inviting green campus, where cyclists and skaters join museum-goers on the plant-bordered paths in fair weather.*

TOP 10 Sights

1 Field Museum
2 John G. Shedd Aquarium
3 Adler Planetarium
4 Prairie Avenue District
5 Blues Heaven Foundation
6 Maxwell Street Market
7 Museum of Contemporary Photography
8 Chinatown
9 National Vietnam Veterans Art Museum
10 Jane Addams' Hull House

Seals, Shedd Aquarium

Field Museum
1 One of the three lakefront institutions to occupy the 57-acre (23-ha) Museum Campus, this vast museum boasts a collection of more than 20 million fascinating natural history and anthropological artifacts *(see pp14–15)*.

John G. Shedd Aquarium
2 The second of the three Museum Campus sights, the Shedd is also one of the oldest public aquariums in the world. Dive in to discover the many treasures of the aquatic world *(see pp22–3)*.

Adler Planetarium
3 This, the first planetarium in the Western Hemisphere, completes the Museum Campus trio. Visit its numerous galleries to walk among the stars, explore the worlds that orbit the Sun, and be enlightened by 1,000 years of astronomical discovery. Don't miss the opportunity to catch the Sky Theater show, which is projected on the 68-ft (21-m) dome of the historic Zeiss planetarium. The virtual reality events in the StarRider Theater are also awe-inspiring, launching you into the outer reaches of space and even give you the chance to interact with the show via a panel in the armrest. *1300 S. Lake Shore Dr. • Map M6 • Open summer (Jun–Sep) 9am–6pm daily (to 9pm Thu & Fri); winter 9:30am–4:30pm Mon–Fri, 9am–4:30pm Sat & Sun; for showtimes call 312-922-7827 • Adm. • DA*

Figurine, Field Museum

Prairie Avenue District
4 Of the wealthy enclaves both north and south of the Chicago River that grew up following the Great Fire of 1871, Prairie Avenue was the most

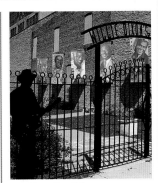

Blues Heaven Foundation

fashionable – and Chicago's ritziest. Only a few of its mansions remain today, of which two are open to the public (by tour only): the imposing, Romanesque-Revival 1887 Glessner House, and Chicago's oldest remaining building – Clarke House – built in 1836 in the Greek-Revival style by New York emigré Henry B. Clarke. *Map C5 • For info on walking tours (May–Oct: 1 & 2pm on 1st & 3rd Sat & Sun) call 312-326-1480 • Clarke House, 1827 S. Indiana Ave., tours noon, 1 & 2pm Wed–Sun, adm., DA • Glessner House, 1800 S. Prairie Ave., tours 1, 2 & 3pm Wed–Sun, adm., no DA*

Blues Heaven Foundation
5 Located in the former studios of Chess Records, where blues greats from Muddy Waters to Willie Dixon once recorded, Blues Heaven has an interesting collection of records, photos, and stage costumes dedicated to Chicago's blues style and its performers. Chess music plays on the PA, and there are occasional live performances. Rock aficionados will note the address is the namesake of a Rolling Stones song. *2120 S. Michigan Ave. • Map C5 • For tours call 312-808-1286 • Closed Sun • Adm. • Limited DA*

Feel like playing the blues? At Blues Heaven Foundation, staff say they can teach visitors the harmonica in 10 minutes.

Fresh produce, Maxwell Street Market

Maxwell Street Market

Both 19th-century European immigrants and 20th-century African-American settlers fleeing the Deep South got their entrepreneurial start selling from push-carts around Maxwell Street. In 1994 the market was relocated to make way for the new University of Illinois at Chicago and, while a shadow of its former self, it still makes for a vibrant Sunday morning. Don't expect valuable finds; do expect plenty of Mexican housewares and used tools. But the occasional treasure, such as a vintage fur coat, does show up. Perhaps the best reason to visit is to try the homemade tacos from the Mexican food stalls that line the street. ⊛ 548 W. Roosevelt Rd. • Map J6 • Open 7am–3pm Sun • Free

Architectural detail, Chinatown

Museum of Contemporary Photography

Run by and located in Columbia College Chicago, this museum is one of a kind in the Midwest. It exhibits the portfolios of international modern masters, with shows (including student shows) tending toward the experimental rather than the traditional documentary. Changing exhibitions also present a healthy mixture of local talents and well-established ones, such as Gary Winogrand and William Eggleston. Frequent gallery talks give curators and artists the chance to discuss the shows with museum-goers. ⊛ 600 S. Michigan Ave. • Map L5 • Open 10am–5pm, Mon–Fri (to 8pm Thu), noon–5pm Sat • Free • DA

Chinatown

Crowned by the landmark Chinatown Gate spanning Wentworth Avenue, Chicago's Chinatown isn't that large – running roughly eight blocks – but it is colorful. Home to Chicago's oldest Asian community, Chinatown was founded in the 19th century by transcontinental railroad workers fleeing West Coast prejudice. It continues to be a place where Cantonese and Mandarin are spoken far more widely than English. Stroll Wentworth to see the ornate On Leong Tong Building, buy fresh almond cookies from Chinese bakeries, peruse the many import and herbal shops, or chow down in one of the dozens of local restaurants. ⊛ Around Wentworth Ave. & Cermak Rd. • Map B5

National Vietnam Veterans Art Museum

A moving tribute to the horrors of war, this museum, started in the late 1970s, now showcases over 1,000 works by more than 130 artists once involved in the conflict. Most of the artworks, which include paintings, sculptures, and drawings, as well as prose and poetry, come from former US soldiers, doctors and

R. R. Yonkha's *This Is How You Died*,
National Vietnam Veterans Art Museum

POWs, though powerful entries
by former Viet Cong and native
Cambodians attest to the universal
effects of the conflict.

Ⓢ *1801 S. Indiana Ave.* • *Map C5*
• *312-326-0270* • *Open 11am–6pm Tue–Fri,*
10am–5pm Sat, noon–5pm Sun • *Adm.*
• *DA* • *Call for visits*

🔟 Jane Addams' Hull House

When European immigrants
were flooding Chicago to work in
its rail and stock yards during the
late 19th and early 20th centuries,
Jane Addams bought Hull House
for a specific purpose. From here,
she offered social services and
facilities to this immigrant working class, including day care,
employment counselling and art
classes. A great social reformer
and winner of the 1931 Nobel
Peace Prize, Addams also cham-
pioned the rights of women and
helped usher in child labor laws.
Her original office, furnishings,
and artwork are still in place for
visitors to see, supplemented by
temporary exhibits that tell the
story of the settlement at Hull
House and the invaluable work
of its residents. Ⓢ *800 S. Halsted St.*
• *Map H5* • *Open 10am– 4pm Tue–Fri,*
noon–4pm Sun • *Free* • *DA*

Exploring South Loop

Morning

Start by grabbing coffee
and an omelet at the boho
Artists' Restaurant (412 S.
Michigan Ave.) From there,
walk down to Balbo Avenue
to catch the free trolley *(see
p108)* that will take you to
Museum Campus. Here
you can chose between the
Field Museum *(see pp14–
15)*, **Adler Planetarium**
(see p93), and **Shedd
Aquarium** *(see pp22–3)* all
within walking distance of
each other. If you plan to
visit other museums on
your trip, it makes sense
to purchase a City Pass
(see p108). If you opt to
see the highlights of each,
end up at the Shedd, where
the **Soundings** restaurant
offers good food and great
views overlooking the lake.

Afternoon

Hail a cab (plenty wait outside the museums) or
walk to the nearby pedes-
trian bridge at 18th Street
to get to the **Prairie
Avenue District** *(see p93)*,
where you can stroll the
historic streets and maybe
even catch the 3pm tour
of the **Glessner House**
(see p93). If you've still
got the energy, walk one
block west to the fasci-
nating **National Vietnam
Veterans Art Museum**.

Evening

Head over to Wabash
Avenue for an early supper
at one of the trendy
eateries on this burgeoning
strip. Mayor Richard Daley
has been known to
frequent **Gioco** *(1312 S.
Wabash Ave., 312-939-
3870)* for its stellar Italian
fare (reservations are
recommended). Ready for
more? Then stay up late to
hear the blues at **Buddy
Guy's Legends** *(see p96)*.

Left **Diners, Hawkeye's Bar & Grill** Right **The Cotton Club**

🔟 Bars & Clubs

1 Buddy Guy's Legends
Run by bluesman Buddy Guy, this club is arguably the city's best. To get a table, come early and dine on decent barbecue. ◈ *754 S. Wabash Ave. • Map K6*

2 Hothouse
Not-for-profit Hothouse serves up a gumbo of music in art-filled digs. Acts range from jazz to Afro-pop, with a smattering of poetry readings and performance art. ◈ *31 E. Balbo Dr. • Map L5*

3 The Cotton Club
In this lively two-room club, the jazz room is modeled on Harlem's famed Cotton Club. In another room DJs spin hip-hop and contemporary beats. ◈ *1710 S. Michigan Ave. • Map L6 • Closed Tue*

4 The Velvet Lounge
Ignore the threadbare decor; The Velvet Lounge offers some of the city's best jazz including jam sessions with the bar's owner, a saxman himself. ◈ *2128 1/2 S. Indiana Ave. • Map L6 • Closed Mon & Tue*

5 NetWorks
A popular gathering place, NetWorks airs news and sports on an array of TVs. ◈ *Hyatt Regency McCormick Place, 2233 S. Martin Luther King Dr. • Map D5 • Free*

6 Mr. Ricky's Note
A smartly dressed, urban professional crowd steps out here for old school R&B. ◈ *118 E Cermak Rd. • Map B5 • Closed Sun & Mon*

7 Bar Louie Taylor
One of several popular Bar Louies in town, this Little Italy outpost plies generous martinis (and great bar food) to a twenty-something crowd. ◈ *1321 W. Taylor St. • Map H6 • Free*

8 Beviamo Wine Bar
This dark, intimate Little Italy hideaway is a great place to cozy as a couple before or after dinner with one of 40 by-the-glass wines, or a "sampling flight" of three wines. ◈ *1358 W. Taylor St. • Map H6 • Free • Closed Sun*

9 Vernon Park Tap
Also known as Tufano's, this popular bar counts legions of local and celebrity fans who pile in for house wine and generous, inexpensive pastas. ◈ *1073 W. Vernon Park Pl. • Map H5 • Free • Closed Mon*

10 Hawkeye's Bar & Grill
Try this sports bar for beer-fueled camaraderie and a genuine slice of Chicago fan zeal. A shuttle bus even delivers patrons to the United Center and US Cellular Field. ◈ *1458 W. Taylor St. • Map H6 • Free • No DA*

Unless otherwise specified bars and clubs charge admission, are open nightly, and have DA.

Price Categories

Price categories include a three-course meal for one, a glass of house wine, tax, and a 15-20% tip.

$	under $20
$$	$20–$30
$$$	$30–$45
$$$$	$45–$60
$$$$$	over $60

Phoenix

🔟 Places to Eat

1 Phoenix
Phoenix attracts dim sum diners from near and far. Go early on weekends or prepare for long waits. ◈ 2131 S. Archer Ave. • Map A6 • 312-328-0848 • $$

2 Opera
Trendsetter Opera serves contemporized Chinese food in a former 1930s warehouse. Don't miss the five-spice squid and slow-braised pork. ◈ 1301 S. Wabash Ave. • Map K6 • 312-461-0161 • Closed lunch • $$$$

3 Gioco
Rustic Italian food is the draw at this stylish restaurant and one-time speakeasy. ◈ 1312 S. Wabash Ave. • Map K6 • 312-939-3870 • Closed lunch Sat & Sun • $$$$

4 Lao Szechuan
Located in the Chinatown Square shopping mall, this simple eaterie serves authentic Chinese Szechuan cuisine. ◈ 2172 S. Archer Ave. • Map C5 • 312-326-5040 • $

5 Chez Joel
A quaint French bistro in the heart of Little Italy charms fans with its sunny decor and fine classics like steak au poivre. ◈ 1119 W. Taylor St. • Map H6 • 312-226-6479 • Closed lunch Sat & Sun • $$$$

6 Pompei Bakery
A top Little Italy lunch pick, Pompeii showcases a dozen varieties of square, by-the-slice pizzas. Hot sandwiches and stuffed pastas round out the offerings. ◈ 1531 W. Taylor St. • Map H6 • 312-421-5179 • No reservations • $

7 Francesca's on Taylor
The Little Italy branch of Wrigleyville's Mia Francesca offers generous portions of refined Italian cuisine at reasonable prices. ◈ 1400 W. Taylor St. • Map H6 • 312-829-2828 • Closed lunch Sat & Sun • $$$

8 Rosebud Cafe
Its Italian cooking isn't daring but Rosebud's convivial vibe is hard to resist. Long waits for tables are common. ◈ 1500 W. Taylor St. • Map H6 • 312-942-1117 • Closed lunch Sat & Sun • $$$

9 Chicago Firehouse
The menu at this former fire station is best at its most basic, including burgers and sandwiches. ◈ 1401 S. Michigan Ave. • Map L6 • 312-786-1401 • Closed lunch Sat & Sun • $$$$

10 Penang
Chicago's only Malaysian restaurant. Ask your server to recommend the best dishes on the menu. ◈ 2201 S. Wentworth Ave. • Map C5 • 312-326-6888 • $$

> *Unless otherwise stated, all restaurants recommend reservations, accept credit cards, have DA, and are open for lunch and dinner.*

Left **South Shore Cultural Center** Right **University of Chicago Campus**

Far South

WITH MAGNIFICENT ARCHITECTURE, *interesting ethnic enclaves, and standout museums, Chicago's Far South encompasses districts such as Hyde Park and Kenwood that merit a journey off the beaten tourist track – despite being bordered to the south by some less-than-welcoming neighborhoods. Hyde Park and Kenwood began life as suburbs for the wealthy escaping the dirty city; today, this part of town is a fascinating melting pot of University of Chicago students and Mexican, Asian, African-American, and Indian residents. Recreation and leisure opportunities abound on spectacular tracts of green space, including the University of Chicago's Midway Plaisance and Jackson Park, site of the 1893 World's Columbian Exposition (see p19).*

🔟 Sights

1. Museum of Science and Industry
2. University of Chicago
3. DuSable Museum of African-American History
4. South Shore Cultural Center
5. Oriental Institute
6. Robie House
7. Kenwood Historic District
8. Washington Park
9. Osaka Japanese Gardens
10. University of Chicago Sculptures

Giant Heart, Museum of Science and Industry

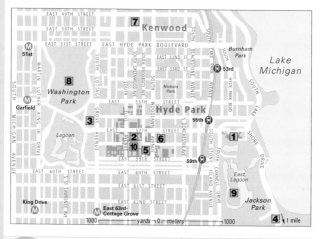

Around Town – Far South

1 Museum of Science and Industry

The largest science museum within a single building in the Western Hemisphere, this museum attracts an amazing two million people a year *(see pp16–19)*.

2 University of Chicago

Noted for its research and high educational standards, this remarkable private university has produced over 70 Nobel Prize winners *(see pp28–9)*.

3 DuSable Museum of African-American History

Located on the eastern edge of the beautiful Washington Park, this museum is named after Chicago's first non-native settler, Jean Baptiste Point du Sable. The permanent exhibits here celebrate other firsts, such as the first black US astronaut, Major Robert Lawrence, and Chicago's first and only African-American mayor, Harold Washington. Thought-provoking exhibits include rusted slave shackles and the "Freedom Now" mural, depicting 400 years of African-American history from the early days of slavery to Civil Rights marches. ⊗ *740 E. 56th Pl. • Map D5 • Open 10am–5pm Mon–Sat, noon–5pm Sun • Adm. (free Sun) • DA*

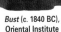

Bust (c. 1840 BC), Oriental Institute

4 South Shore Cultural Center

How ironic that this bustling arts and community center, which serves a largely African-American demographic, began in 1905 as an exclusive country club that barred minority members. Designed by the team who later worked on the elegant Drake Hotel *(see*

Annie Malone exhibit, Dusable Museum

p115), this grand Mediterranean-style structure was bought and lovingly restored by the Chicago Park District when the country club fizzled out in the 1970s. Extravagant landscaping and flower beds complete the pretty picture, making it a popular spot for weddings and festivals, as well as for all kinds of performances and classes. Its golf course, nature park, and the public beach behind it add to its many draws. ⊗ *7059 S. Shore Dr. • Map F6 • Open 9am–6pm Mon–Fri, 9am–5pm Sat • Free (except classes) • DA*

5 Oriental Institute

Learn about the origins of agriculture, the invention of writing, the birth of civilization, and the beginning of the study of arts, science, politics, and religion at this University of Chicago departmental museum. Its five galleries showcase ancient Near Eastern civilizations from about 3500 BC to AD 100, and the exhibits were largely unearthed during the department's own excavations. ⊗ *1155 E. 58th St. • Map E6 • 10am–6pm Tue–Sat (to 8:30pm Wed), noon–6pm Sun • Free • DA*

Robie House

6 This splendid 1909 residence by Frank Lloyd Wright is easily spotted by its steel-beam roof, which overhangs the building by 20 ft (6 m) at each end. Take a tour through its low-ceilinged interior, and

Frank Lloyd Wright tables and chairs in Robie House

past more than 170 art-glass windows and doors, to gain insight into the ongoing, extensive ten-year restoration program. The building was a private home until 1926, when it became a dormitory for the Chicago Theological Seminary. It was later bought by a development firm, who donated it to the University of Chicago in 1963, the same year it was designated a National Historic Landmark. ◈ 5757 S. Woodlawn Ave. • Map E6 • Tours by appointment only, call: 1-773-834-1847 • Adm. • No DA

Kenwood Historic District

7 A world apart from some of the Far South's dicier areas, this wealthy enclave within Kenwood, founded by John A. Kennicott in 1856, has mansions that have to be seen to be believed. In the late 19th century, this area was an upscale Chicago suburb, where wealthy residents built majestic homes on spacious lots, a rarity in the quickly booming city. A stroll around the district will uncover architectural styles ranging from Italianate and Colonial Revival to Prairie style, by influential figures such as Howard Van Doren Shaw and Frank Lloyd Wright (see pp30–31). ◈ Boundaries: E. 43rd St. (north), E. 51st St. (south), S. Blackstone Ave. (east), and S. Drexel Blvd. (west) • Map E5

Washington Park

8 Frederick Law Olmsted and Calvert Vaux, the designers of New York's Central Park, also created this 371-acre (150-ha) green space for Chicago residents in the early 1870s. It originally attracted mainly wealthy city dwellers who enjoyed parading around the scenic space. Today, it's a beautiful and widely used park with recreational programs, the DuSable Museum of African-American History, and Lorado Taft's striking 110-ft (34-m) long sculpture, *Fountain of Time*, which took him 14 years to build. It is unwise to venture into the park after dark.

Detail of Taft's *Fountain of Time*, Washington Park

◈ Map D5 • Open dawn–11pm (approx) • Free • DA

Osaka Japanese Gardens

9 At the north end of Jackson Park's serene Wooded Island (which is excellent for bird-watching), lies this hushed retreat, complete with meandering paths, lagoons, and fountains. The extraordinary garden is a partial re-creation of the one formed in 1934 around the beautiful Japanese Pavilion that had been built for the 1893 Expo, but which sadly burned down in 1946. The gardens were renamed in 1993 for one of

For more on Frank Lloyd Wright architecture See pp30–31

Chicago's sister cities, Osaka, which donated the Japanese gate seen here. ◈ *Jackson Park, 58th St. & Lake Shore Dr.* • *Map F6* • *Open dawn–11pm (approx)* • *Free* • *DA*

10 University of Chicago Sculptures

Strolling around the University of Chicago campus, there's more of visual interest than its buildings alone. Over the years, the university has acquired around 12 outdoor sculptures, including Wolf Vostell's whimsical 1970 *Concrete Traffic*, a car embedded in concrete at the southwest end of the Midway Plaisance and the sobering *Nuclear Energy*, a bronze by Henry Moore that resembles a mushroom cloud. Set within a reflecting pool at 60th Street and University Avenue is *Construction in Space in the Third and Fourth Dimension*, a soaring abstract piece created in the 1950s by Constructivist Antoine Pevsner, which visually depicts the space-time continuum *(see p28–9).*

Osaka Japanese Gardens

For more on Chicago parks and gardens See pp62–3

Exploring Far South

Morning

🕙 Mingle with University of Chicago students over good coffee and great pancakes at the **Original Pancake House** *(see p103)*, where the sweet, baked Apple Dutch Baby is a must-try. From there, walk about a mile (1.6 km) south or hop on the no. 28 bus at the corner of Hyde Park Boulevard and Lake Park Avenue to visit the **Museum of Science & Industry** *(see pp16–19)*, where you can easily spend an engrossing few hours exploring the hands-on exhibits. For lunch, skip the museum food and head west about a mile (1.6 km) to **Medici** *(see p103)*, a great Italian joint, known for its delicious pizzas. The extravagant Garbage Pizza is a favorite.

Afternoon

Stroll about four blocks southwest to the **Oriental Institute** *(see p99)* at the **University of Chicago** *(see pp28–9)* whose museum will transport you back to ancient times. Its Suq gift shop offers unique souvenirs, such as a replica of an ancient board game. Just east of the institute is Frank Lloyd Wright's masterpiece of Prairie-style architecture, **Robie House**. Take a tour of this to really gain some insight into the great man's vision. Then stroll around the university's leafy quadrangles if it's good weather, or backtrack a little to the **Smart Museum of Art** *(see p28)* if you'd rather be inside. Either way, round off your day with some good ol' home-style Southern cooking at the no-frills **Dixie Kitchen** *(see p103)*.

Left **Leather shoes, Collections** Right **House of Africa**

Shops

1 Powell's Bookstore
Here, used books in top condition are stacked floor to ceiling on painted wood shelves, with antique editions protected behind glass. ❧ *1501 E. 57th St. • Map E6*

2 Seminary Co-op Bookstore
Housed in the basement of the Chicago Theological Seminary on the University of Chicago campus, it's fitting that this bookstore has a well-respected academic section, especially humanities and social sciences. ❧ *5757 S. University Ave. • Map E5*

3 57th Street Books
This basement-level shop carries new fiction, children's books, and African-American interest titles. Low ceilings, brick walls, and a painted cement floor all create a cozy atmosphere, conducive to browsing.
❧ *1301 E. 57th St. • Map E6 • No DA*

4 The Co-op Market
Mingle with the melting pot of shoppers at this cooperative market, where aisles are dominated by organic, vegetarian, and international foodstuffs. ❧ *1526 E. 55th Street • Map E5*

5 House of Africa
The scent of sandlewood incense fills this small boutique that sells African artifacts, carved wooden sculptures, and CDs of music from all over the continent.
❧ *1352 E. 53rd St. • Map E5 • Closed Sun*

6 2nd Hand Tunes
In this long, narrow, cement-block store, rows of LPs, 45s, and CDs attract local music lovers and club DJs for the outstanding collection of soul, jazz, and indie rock. ❧ *1377 E. 53rd St. • Map E5*

7 Toys, Etc.
This inviting store focuses on non-violent toys galore. Good-old standbys include kites, face-painting kits, balls, and dress-up clothes. ❧ *5211 S. Harper Ave. • Map F5*

8 Little Black Pearl Workshop
Tucked away in a limestone rowhouse, the gift shop at this children's arts program sells the students' amazing creations, such as one-of-kind painted furniture and vibrant mosaics. ❧ *4200 S. Drexel Blvd. • Map E5 • Closed Sat & Sun*

9 Collections
Chic club clothes and look-at-me leather shoes are sparsely displayed along the walls in this boutique. Many of the designs are straight off Italian runways, while others are custom-made by the shop's owner.
❧ *1360 E. 53rd St. • Map E5 • Closed Sun*

10 Artisans 21
This gallery showcases locally made art. You can purchase designs both to wear and to show, from whimsical ceramics to fringed silk scarves and handpainted jackets. ❧ *5225 S. Harper • Map F5 • No DA*

Most of these shops are usually open at least 10am–6pm Mon–Sat and noon–5pm Sun, and unless specified have DA

Price Categories

Price categories in-
clude a three-course
meal for one, a glass
of house wine, tax,
and a 15–20% tip.

$	under $20
$$	$20–$30
$$$	$30–$45
$$$$	$45–$60
$$$$$	over $60

Dixie Kitchen and Bait Shop

🔟 Places to Eat

1 La Petite Folie
An upscale French restau-
rant offering a fixed-price menu,
as well as entrées featuring ingredients such as rabbit and quail.
Ⓢ *1504 E. 55th St. • Map E5 • 1-773-493-
1394 • Closed Mon, Sat & Sun lunch • $$$*

2 Florian Caffé
This no-reservations hangout
for pizza and pasta also specializes
in mile-high cakes, rich with
chocolate, strawberry, coconut,
and thick frosting. Ⓢ *1450 E. 57th
St. • Map E6 • 1-773-752-4100 • $$*

3 Calypso Café
In this feel-good Caribbean
joint, jerk chicken is a favorite, and
Key Lime pie is the must-do
dessert. Ⓢ *5211 S. Harper St. • Map
H6 • 1-773-955-0229 • $$*

4 Dixie Kitchen & Bait Shop
A taste of America's South,
serving fried catfish, crawfish
étouffée, and jambalaya in a
setting reminiscent of an old bait
shop. Ⓢ *5225 S. Harper Ave. • Map F5
• 1-773-363-4943 • $$*

5 Medici on 57th
Great pizza draws the crowds,
but sandwiches on home-baked
bread and rich milkshakes are
also offered. Ⓢ *1327 E. 57th St.
• Map E6 • 1-773-667-7394 • $$*

6 Cedars of Lebanon
Delicious falafel, lamb
kebobs, hummus, and dozens of
other Middle Eastern dishes will
fill you up for next to nothing at
this BYO spot. Ⓢ *Kimbark Plaza, 1618
E. 53rd St. • Map E5 • 1-773-324-6227 • $*

7 Nile Restaurant
The extensive menu at this
Middle Eastern diner makes
decisions difficult, but combination
plates let you try an assortment.
Ⓢ *1611 E. 55th St. • Map E5 • 1-773-324-
9499 • $ • No DA*

8 Woodlawn Tap
A casual dress code, good
food, and cheap beer attract all
types to this bar especially for
burgers and hearty soup. Ⓢ *1172 E.
55th St. • Map E5 • 1-773-643-5516 • $$*

9 Mellow Yellow
This laid-back eatery offers
specialties of rotisserie chicken
and sweet or savory crepes.
There's also a separate bar.
Ⓢ *1508 E. 53rd St. • Map E5 • 1-773-667-
2000 • $*

10 Original Pancake House
This homey breakfast haven
does everything well, but its signature dish is the apple pancake.
Ⓢ *1517 E. Hyde Park Ave. • Map E5
• 1-773-288-2322 • Closed dinner • $*

*Unless otherwise stated, all restaurants recommend reservations,
accept credit cards, have DA, and are open for lunch and dinner.*

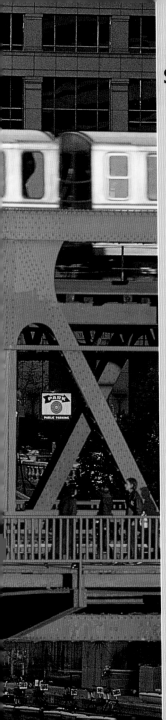

STREETSMART

CHICAGO'S TOP 10

Left **Christmas lights** Center **Wrapping up warmly** Right **Spring Tulips, Magnificent Mile**

Planning Your Trip

1 When to Go
If you prefer a moderate climate, the best time to visit Chicago is spring or fall. But if you can bear the snow and bitter cold of the festive season, you'll see the city sparkle with magical Christmas lights – and you'll have a lot fewer tourists to contend with. Avoid November visits, as the city's hotels are filled by conventioneers during this month.

2 Weather
Chicago winters are usually intemperate with heavy snow and temperatures ranging from 13° F (-9° C) to 37° F (4° C). Summer days can be anything from balmy to boiling, averaging 69° F (22° C) to 84° F (30° C). Extremes, like winter blizzards, heavy spring rains, and summer heat waves are not uncommon, with spring-time weather being particularly changeable. Despite the winds that can gust off Lake Michigan, Chicago's "Windy City" moniker is actually attributed to the verbose bid the city made to host the 1893 World's Columbian Exposition *(see p19)*.

3 What to Pack
Pack lightly for summer, and bring layers for the unpredictable spring and fall conditions. Layers are best for the often desperately cold winters, in order to cope with centrally heated environments. A hat and suitable footwear are essential then too. While casual clothes are acceptable in most places, men should bring a jacket and tie, since they are required at many upscale restaurants.

4 Insurance
It is strongly recommended to have a comprehensive travel insurance policy, including coverage for trip cancellation, lost luggage, car rental insurance and, most of all, medical expenses, which are very high in America.

5 Passports & Visas
Citizens of European Union countries, New Zealand, Australia, and Japan can spend up to 90 days in the US without a visa. They just need a valid passport and a round-trip ticket. Canadian citizens must only show photo ID and proof of residence. Citizens of other countries should contact their local US embassy well in advance of their trip to obtain the relevant visa.

6 Money
Do bring some dollars with you for essentials on arrival. But from then on, major credit cards are accepted in most places. ATMs abound, but check with your own bank to avoid the extra fee charged for using ATMs of non-affiliated US banks. It's also worthwhile bringing a few US dollar traveler's checks in case of emergency. These can be changed at most banks and foreign exchange on showing photo ID, and can also be used in stores and restaurants.

7 Driver's License
Foreign or out-of-state driver's licenses are valid in Chicago – if they are in English. Bring your picture license even if you don't plan to rent a car: it's a good alternative to a passport if you are asked for proof of age in a bar.

8 Electric Current & Phone Adapters
Electrical appliances in US operate on 110–120 volts and use two-prong plugs. This means that non-US, single-voltage appliances need an adapter and transformer, available in airport shops, and at many electrical stores and large department stores.

9 Discounts
If you have student or senior ID, it's a good idea to carry it with you to make the best of discounts offered on everything from public transit and hotels to admission to the main attractions.

10 Time Zone
Chicago operates on Central Time (six hours behind GMT). Daylight saving begins at 3am on the first Sunday in April and reverts to standard time at 1am on the last Sunday in October.

Left **Blue Line Train sign** Center **Amtrak train** Right **O'Hare Airport**

TOP 10 Arriving in Chicago

1 O'Hare International Airport

One of the world's busiest airports, O'Hare lies 20 miles (32 km) northwest of downtown Chicago. Serving most major airlines, this airport is big and spread out. Use the free Airport Transport System (ATS) to access the three domestic terminals, the international terminal, parking areas, and the Metra *(see p108)* station. ● *1-800-832-6352, www.ohare.com*

2 Connections from O'Hare

Taxis are available on a first come first served basis from the lower level of the Arrivals terminal. Out of rush hours it can take around 45 minutes to reach Downtown. Car rental agencies are also at hand, near the baggage claim areas in terminals 1–3, and via courtesy telephones from terminal 5. Alternatively, shuttle buses, limos, and trains can take you into Chicago. For the latter, follow the "Trains to City" signs to the Chicago Transit Authority (CTA) Blue Line, the cheapest and – at 40 minutes – often the quickest way into town.

3 Midway Airport

Located 10 miles (16 km) southwest of Downtown, this recently renovated airport serves mostly budget airlines, as well as a few major ones. Taxis are available from

exit M5; car rental agencies are located in the main terminal building; and shuttle buses leave from in front of it. Alternatively, follow signs from the terminal to the CTA station: the Orange Line brings you downtown in less than 30 minutes. ● *1-773-838-0600*

4 Immigration

Landing cards and customs forms are distributed on the plane. Foreign nationals have to join a separate line to have these and their passports inspected after landing. Strict security checks, involving the taking of photographs and fingerprints, are now in place for those arriving in the US on a visa.

5 Shuttle Buses

These operate from both airports. Continental Airport Express will drop off at (and pick up from) any requested downtown location: Omega Airport Shuttle buses operate between the two airports. To catch a shuttle, go to the information counter at Baggage Claims. ● *Continental Airport Express: 1-888-284-3826 • Omega Airport Shuttle: 1-773-483-6634*

6 Limousines

Several limo companies, including Amm's and Chicago Express Limousine, offer private door-to-door services: book 24 hours in advance. Rates are higher than taxi

fares, and tips should be 10–15%. ● *Amm's: 1-773-792-1126 • Chicago Express Limousine: 1-866-691-6010*

7 Car Rental

You usually have to be over 25 with a valid license to rent a car. Reputable agencies such as *Avis* (800-331-1212) and *Hertz* (800-654-3131) are at both main airports and throughout the city. A deposit will be required. Collision damage waiver and liability insurance are highly recommended.

8 By Train

Over 40 Amtrak trains serve Union Station each day. The nearest El stop is at Clinton, but it's a good walk, so it's often better to take a cab or bus to your destination. ● *210 S. Canal St., 1-800-872-7245*

9 By Bus

Catch long-distance buses from Greyhound's main downtown terminal. Then catch a cab to your destination, or walk one block north to take the El from Clinton station. ● *630 W. Harrison St., 1-800-231-2222*

10 By Car

Interstate highways into Chicago are I-55 from the southwest, I-57 from the south, I-88 from the west, I-90 from the east and northwest, and I-94 from the east and north. Route 66 from Santa Monica, CA joins I-55 before hitting Downtown.

Left **Water Taxi** Center **Trolley Bus** Right **Cyclists on the lakefront path**

Getting Around

1 The El
Short for elevated train, the El is nevertheless the name given to the entire CTA-run train network, including the sections that travel underground. The five major and two minor lines are identifiable by color: red, green, blue, brown, orange, purple, and yellow. Some lines run 24 hours a day (less often off-peak). Trains arrive every 5–20 minutes, and the service is fast and economical.
🛈 CTA: 1-888-968-7282 www.transitchicago.com

2 Buses
The CTA also operates an extensive network of buses, especially useful for reaching the lakefront, which is not served by the El. Look for the blue and white stops. Some also serve PACE buses that cover the city suburbs and are numbered 208 and higher.
🛈 CTA: as above • PACE: 1-847-364-7223 www.pacebus.com

3 CTA tickets & passes
A regular El or bus fare is $1.75, with an extra 25¢ for a transfer card (valid for two transfers within two hours of purchase), and you need exact change. However if you buy a Transit card with a preset value at a station ticket office, or get a top-up Transit card and charge it with the desired amount at a machine, the relevant fare is then deducted from your pass each time you take a ride. One- to five-day Visitor Passes are also available from stations, visitor centers, and selected tourist attractions.

4 Metra
Metra, the commuter rail system, serves the city's suburbs. Fares vary according to the journey's length. Downtown stops are Union Station, LaSalle Street Station, Ogilvie Transportation Center (see p37), and Randolph Street Station. 🛈 Metra: 312-322-6777 (Mon–Fri), www.metrarail.com

5 Taxis
It is usually easy to hail a cab Downtown. Elsewhere, it's better to call for one. There's an intial charge, then a fee per mile and per extra passenger. A 10–15% tip is expected. Companies include: 🛈 Checker Taxi Assoc. 312-243-2537 • Flash Cab Co. 1-773-561-1444 • Yellow Cab Co. 312-829-3576

6 Water Taxis
In summer, Wendella Riverbus (312-337-1446) runs water taxis between the Wrigley Building and both Union Station and the Ogilvie Transportaion Center. Shoreline Water Taxi (312-222-9328) also offers a service every 20 minutes from Navy Pier (see pp20–21) to the John G. Shedd Aquarium and near the Sears Tower.

7 Trolley Buses
From Memorial Day to Labor Day (see 109), free daytime trolley buses run on four routes from downtown El and Metra stations to the Museum Campus, the Art Institute of Chicago, State Street and Michigan Avenue shopping areas, Navy Pier – and on weekends they run to Lincoln Park and Chinatown/Pilsen (see pp52–3). 🛈 1-877-2442246, www.877chicago.com

8 Walking
Exploring compact areas (such as the Mag Mile and Lincoln Park) on foot is great in fine weather. However, avoid walking alone after dark.

9 Cycling
Only confident cyclists should consider city cycling as the roads are so busy. However, the 18 miles (29 km) of lakefront bike paths are very pleasant. To get a Chicago Bike Map call 312-742-2453. Bike Chicago rents bikes and conducts bike tours from Navy Pier: call 1-800-915-2453 or visit www.bikechicago.com

10 Driving
Chicago's grid system (see street index), makes orientation relatively straightforward. However, expressways are often snarled, the Loop's one-way streets can be very confusing, and finding parking Downtown can be a huge, costly problem.

Left **No smoking sign** Center **Visitors Information center** Right **Disabled sign**

Useful Information

1 Information Centers

Chicago has three main tourist information centers: in the Chicago Cultural Center (see p69); in the Historic Pumping Station (see p26), and at Navy Pier (see pp20–21). Opening hours are at least 10am–5pm. You can also get further information by contacting the Chicago Convention and Tourism Bureau (312-201-8847), or get in touch with the Illinois Bureau of Tourism (1-800-226-6632).

2 Websites

Information about Chicago can be found on several reliable websites, such as www. choose chicago.com and www. 877chicago.com. For in-depth reviews of where to go and what to see, log onto www.metromix.com, affiliated to the Chicago Tribune. Internet cafés include the national chain Screenz (773-348-9300).

3 Media

The city's two main daily newspapers are the Chicago Tribune and the Chicago Sun-Times. The most popular radio stations include: WNUA (95.5 FM) for jazz, WFMT (98.7 FM) for classical, WLUP (97.9 FM) for rock, and WGCI (107.5 FM) for R&B. WBBM (780 AM) is a news station, and WSCR (670 AM) keeps you up to date on sports. As for local TV, there's a wide range to choose from:

CBS (Channel 2); NBC (Channel 5); ABC (Channel 7); WB (Channel 9); WTTW Public TV (Channel 11); and Fox (Channel 32).

4 Events

For a complete list of what's on in Chicago see www.877chicago.com, or pick up the Chicago Reader – a free paper that comes out every Thursday, available in restaurants, bars, and other venues. Chicago is known for its conventions, some so large that conventioneers almost take over the city. Check the "Convention Calendar" at www.choose chicago.com, to see if your visit coincides with any.

5 Tipping

Plan to tip for most services. Waitstaff expect 15–20 percent; bell hops and porters $1 per bag, hotel maids around $2 per night, and bartenders up to $1 per drink.

6 Telephones

Most public phones accept coins or phone cards (calls to Directory Assistance are free). Within Chicago you need to dial the area code 312. Otherwise, dial a 1 in front of all other US codes. To dial abroad, key 011 + country code + city code (omitting any initial 0). If you need to rent a cell phone, try International Sound (1-800-353-2100). AT&T, Nextel, and Sprint are the largest mobile service providers.

7 Families & Disabled Visitors

Chicago Parent magazine (www.chicagoparent.com) has a monthly calendar of kids' activities. Access Chicago, published by the Mayor's Office, provides information on handicap accessibility to the city's main attractions. Call 312-744-7050 to obtain a copy.

8 Smoking & Drinking

Smoking is prohibited in many public spaces in Chicago, so check for no smoking signs before lighting up. The legal age for the purchase or consumption of alcohol is 21, and the law requires photo ID as proof.

9 Consulates

In emergencies, your consulate may give assistance. ⊗ Australia: 123 N. Wacker Dr., 312-419-1480 • Canada: 180 N. Stetson Ave., 312-616-1860 • Great Britain: Wrigley Building, 400 N. Michigan Ave., 312- 970-3800 • Ireland: 400 N. Michigan Ave, 312-337-1868

10 Public Holidays

New Year's Day (Jan 1); Martin Luther King Day (3rd Mon in Jan); President's Day (3rd Mon in Feb); Casimir Pulaski Day (1st Mon in Mar); Memorial Day (last Mon in May); Independence Day (July 4); Labor Day (1st Mon in Sep); Thanksgiving (4th Thu in Nov); Christmas Day (Dec 25).

Left **Lakefront recreation** Center **Hot Tix sign** Right **Public Art, North Michigan Avenue**

TOP 10 Chicago on a Budget

1 Free Admission Days
Several city attractions such as Lincoln Park Zoo *(see p24–5)* never charge admission. Others often have one free day per week: bear in mind it might be cheaper, but the crowds can be greater.

2 Free Events
Summer in Chicago brings sunshine and lots of free outdoor happenings, especially in Grant Park *(see p71)*. Arrive early to get a good spot, and bring a picnic and warm clothing for after the sun goes down. The Mayor's Office of Special Events and other sources of information *(see p109)* will have details of concerts, neighborhood festivals, parades, and more. ✆ *Mayor's Office of Special Events (recorded info) • 312-744-3370 • www.cityof chicago.org/specialevents*

3 Free Tours
The Chicago Office of Tourism *(see p109)* provides information on a range of great free tours, such as the Cultural Center Tour and the Loop Tour Train *(see p111)*. The volunteer-run Chicago Greeters also offers an insider's take on the city at no charge *(see p111)*.

4 Dining Deals
Many restaurants have good-value "Early Bird Specials" or "pre-theater menus." Look for signs advertising deals.

5 Hot Tix
Half-price tickets for same-day theater performances can be bought in person at Hot Tix booths around the city. There is a slight discount for cash payment and a small fee for ticket processing. To save time fruitlessly waiting in line, check the website for daily listings of availability. ✆ *Hot Tix: Chicago Cultural Center, 78 W. Randolph St.• Hot Tix: Waterworks Visitor Center 163 E. Pearson St. • Hot Tix: Tower Records (closed Sun): 214 S. Wabash Ave. & 2301 N. Clark St. • All closed Mon. • www.hottix.org*

6 Public Art
Many famous artists, such as Pablo Picasso and Marc Chagall, have left their artistic mark on the city. Details of public art Downtown are included in a free booklet, the *Loop Sculpture Guide*, which is available at the Chicago Cultural Center and the Waterworks Visitor Center. The University of Chicago *(see pp28–9)* also has notable works on campus, while Navy Pier has sculpture displays during summer.

7 Parks & Recreation
Chicago's many beautiful parks are run by the Chicago Park District. Their excellent facilities include skating areas, beaches, pools, golf courses, tennis courts, and walking and cycling paths. Contact Bike Chicago *(see p111)* at Navy Pier to rent bikes or in-line skates. ✆ *Chicago Park District: 312-742-7529, www.chicagoparkdistrict.com*

8 TV Audience Tickets
Free tickets for the *Oprah* and *Jerry Springer* shows are in demand, so call the hotlines at least a month in advance to avoid disappointment. Audience members generally have to be 18 years of age or over. ✆ *Oprah: Harpo Studios, 1058 W. Washington St., 312-591-9222 • Jerry Springer: NBC Tower, 454 N. Columbus Dr., 312-321-5365, www.studio audiences.com/daytime*

9 Special Promotions
Throughout the year, the Chicago Office of Tourism *(see p109)* offers several promotions, such as Winter Delights, which include discounts on lodging, attractions, and meals.

10 CityPass
This pass grants entry to the Museum Campus trio *(see p93)*; The Art Institute of Chicago; John Hancock Observatory; Museum of Science & Industry; Field Museum; and Shedd Aquarium. It can be purchased online or at any of the participating venues, and is valid for nine days from the first day of use. It offers substantial savings, and you don't have to wait in line. ✆ *www.citypass.com*

Left **Uptown's Argyle Street Neighborhood** Center **Carriage Tours** Right **Lake Michigan Tours**

Tours & Cruises

1 Chicago Neighborhood Tours

Apart from tours of neighborhoods such as Chinatown and Bronzeville, this company also runs special interest bus trips (on themes like Chicago's theaters). Tours begin at the Chicago Cultural Center *(see p69)*: call ahead to book. ◈ *Chicago Neighborhood Tours: 312-742-1190, www.chgocitytours.com*

2 Chicago Architectural Foundation Tours

Learn about the city's amazing architecture on a Chicago Architecture Foundation (CAF) walking, bike, bus, or (in summer) boat tour. The fascinating trips highlight both historic and modern buildings, including Frank Lloyd Wright's architectural legacy. ◈ *CAF: 224 S. Michigan Ave., 312-922-8687, www.architecture.org*

3 Bike Chicago Tours

Bike Chicago will guide you through the city's beautiful parks, neighborhoods, or along the stunning lakefront departing from either of its two locales. ◈ *Navy Pier: 600 E. Grand Ave., 312-595-9600 • North Avenue Beach: 1-773-327-2706 • www.bikechicago.com*

4 Gangster Tours

Follow the trails of some of the city's most infamous 1920s and '30s gangster residents. Sites visited on this two-hour tour include that of the St. Valentine's Massacre, Little Italy, and other haunts of the likes of Al Capone and John Dillinger. ◈ *Untouchables: 1-773-881-1195, www.gangstertour.com*

5 Kayak Tours

Exercise your mind and your muscles by kayaking down the Chicago River while learning about the city's history and architecture. There are gangster and ghost themed tours for both beginners and advanced paddlers. ◈ *Wateriders Adventure Agents: 312-953-9287, www.adventure-agents.com*

6 Lake & River Boat Tours

Join a narrated tour from the Lake or Wendella boat tour to gain historical or architectural insight from a different perspective. Metro Ducks offer a wackier take with their tours onboard an amphibious WWII craft. ◈ *Lake Boat Tours: 312-527-1977, www.chicagoline.com • Wendella Boats: 312-337-1446, www.wendellaboats.com • Metro Ducks: 1-800-298-1506, www.metroducks.com/chicago*

7 Chicago Greeters

Run by the Chicago Office of Tourism *(see p109)*, this free service gives groups of 1 to 6 visitors a chance to benefit from the wisdom of enthusiastic local residents who know and love the city. Choose from a range of themed or neighborhood tours, and preferably book online seven days in advance. ◈ *312-744-8000, www.chicagogreeter.com*

8 Loop Train Tour

While circling the Loop *(see pp68–75)* on an El train *(see p69)* an expert from the CAF explains the history of significant buildings and the El itself. Free tickets are available at the Chicago Cultural Center *(see p69)* information desk on a first-come, first-served basis each day. ◈ *www.architecture.org, Sat only, May–Sept*

9 Carriage Tours

For a romantic ride along the waterfront, the Mag Mile, or around the Gold Coast area, flag down or book a traditional horse-drawn carriage. A flat fee is charged for a half-hour tour. ◈ *Antique Coach & Carriage: 1-773-735-9400, www.antiquecoach-carriage.com*

10 Lake Cruises

Enjoy a meal or cocktails and dancing onboard the elegant *Odyssey* or *Spirit of Chicago* cruisers. In summer, schooners *Windy I* and *Windy II*, also sail on the breeze. All depart from Navy Pier. ◈ *Odyssey: 1-888-741-0281, www.odysseycruises.com • Spirit of Chicago: 312-836-7899, www.spiritcruises.com • Windy I & II: 312-595-5555, www.tallshipwindy.com*

Left **Osco Drug store** Center **Lake front in Winter** Right **Police**

Tips on Health & Security

1 Preventing Theft
As in most cities, the most common crimes are pickpocketing and purse snatching. Common sense can help deter these problems. Leave surplus cash, unnecessary credit cards, and valuables in a safe place at your hotel. Don't walk around with your wallet in a back pocket, and keep bags securely fastened and close to your body. Do keep a copy of your credit card numbers (and the number to call if they are lost) separate from the cards, and bring photocopies of important documents in case they are stolen.

2 Public Transport
It's best to avoid using public transportation late at night. Take a taxi instead. However, when you do take a train, stand well back on the platform until the train has stopped, never sit in an empty carriage, and do not lean against the train doors. Train platforms and trains usually have an intercom in case of emergency.

3 Knowing Your Surroundings
Plan your route before setting off so that you know where you are going. If you do get lost, try not to make a big show of consulting your map or guidebook. At night, avoid walking alone in dimly lit areas and in parks. Steer clear of areas beyond the

south branch of the Chicago River (west of Downtown) and parts of the South Side where crime levels are higher.

4 Hotel Room Safety
Make yourself aware of the fire escape route from your room as soon as you arrive. Always keep the door locked, and be sure you know who is knocking before you let anyone in. Valuables are best kept locked in the in-room, or preferably hotel, safe.

5 Telephone Hotlines
For police, fire, and medical emergencies call 911. If you are not in a position to speak, the emergency locator should still be able to track you. For non-emergency police matters, such as theft, dial 311 to reach the City Helpline. Both numbers can be accessed by cell phones.

6 Hospitals
Hospitals and emergency rooms are listed in the Yellow Pages of the telephone directory. Your concierge will know which one is most convenient. Weiss Memorial Hospital and Northwestern Memorial Hospital are convenient to Downtown and the north side of the city, while Bernard A. Mitchell Hospital, at the University of Chicago, serves the South Side. ✪ *Weiss Memorial Hospital: 4646 N. Marine Dr., Map B3,*

1-773-878-8700 • Northwestern Memorial Hospital: 251 E. Erie St., Map L2, 312-926-5188 • Bernard A. Mitchell Hospital: 5815 S. Maryland Ave., Map E6, 1-773-702-1000

7 Medical Emergencies
In an emergency, call 911 or go directly to the nearest hospital. Even with medical insurance, you may have to pay for services yourself and claim reimbursement after. Contact your insurer before receiving any treatment.

8 Dental Emergencies
Many dental clinics are open 24 hours. Check with the hotel concierge or contact the Chicago Dental Society for a referral. ✪ *Chicago Dental Society: 312-836-7300*

9 Pharmacies
Pharmacies are plentiful throughout the city. Many are open 24 hours. The most popular drug store chains (Walgreens, Osco, and CVS) all have pharmacies inside.

10 Seasonal Hazards
Chicago is a city of extreme seasons. Visitors should be prepared for cold, windy, and snowy winters, which can create hazardous conditions. In summer, the extreme heat can cause health problems: ensure you apply sunscreen, wear a hat, and drink plenty of water.

Left **Broadway Antique Market** Right **Water Tower Place**

10 Shopping Tips

1 Store Hours
Regular store and mall hours are usually 10am to 9pm, Monday to Saturday, and 11am to 6pm Sunday. However, Northside boutiques and stores along the Mag Mile *(see pp26–7)* often stay open 'til 7–8pm.

2 Taxes
Chicago state and local sales taxes are among the highest in the country at 8.75 percent on all non-food items.

3 Sales Periods
Some Chicago stores have items on sale all year round, but expect real bargains after Christmas, on Presidents' Day, and on Labor Day *(see p109)*.

4 Department Stores
You're in shopper's heaven when it comes to department stores in Chicago, which are mostly located on North Michigan Avenue and State Street. They include upscale Marshal Field's *(see p74)*, practical Carson Pirie Scott & Co. *(see p72)*, traditional Lord & Taylor, and stylish Bloomingdale's Home & Furniture Store *(see p59)*. ◈ *Lord & Taylor: Water Tower Place, 835 N. Michigan Ave. • Bloomingdale's: 900 N. Michigan Ave.*

5 Shopping Malls
There's no shortage of malls in the city, especially vertical ones on the Mag Mile. Here you'll find Water Tower Place *(see p28)*; Westfield North Bridge *(see pp56–7)*; Chicago Place – featuring the Midwest's flagship Saks Fifth Avenue – and 900 North Michigan Shops. Regular malls are scattered all around the city and its suburbs. ◈ *Chicago Place: 700 N. Michigan Ave.*

6 Chicago Souvenirs
Accent on Chicago and the City of Chicago Store have shelves filled with Chicago mementos *(see p59)*. Authentic local food such as pizza and Eli's cheesecake can be shipped anywhere in the US by Taste of Chicago. ◈ *Accent on Chicago: 875 N. Michigan Ave. • City of Chicago Store: Chicago Waterworks Visitors Center, 163 E. Pearson St. • Taste of Chicago: 1-877-908-2783, www.tastesofchicago.com*

7 Discount Outlets
Look for real bargains at Filene's Basement, while higher-end men's and women's clothing are discounted in the Mark Shale and Gap stores. Good value jewelery can be found at the Jeweler's Center *(see p74)*, and cheap housewares at Crate & Barrel. ◈ *Filene's Basement: 1 N. State St./ 830 N. Michigan Ave. • Mark Shale Outlet: 2593 Elston Ave. • Gap Outlet: 2778 N. Milwaukee Ave. • Crate & Barrel Outlet: 1864 N. Clybourn Ave.*

8 Music & Books
Borders and Barnes & Noble bookstores are all over the city. But for specialty books and personal service, try the Savvy Traveller or Sandmeyer's Bookstore. The Virgin Megastore looks cool inside, but Tower Records has a far greater selection. For great value CDs try the back wall racks of the legendary Rolling Stones shop, or go to Second Hand Tunes for used records. ◈ *Savvy Traveller: 310 S. Michigan Ave. • Sandmeyer's Bookstore: 714 S. Dearborn St. • Virgin Megastore: 540 N. Michigan Ave. • Tower Records: 2301 N. Clark St. • Rolling Stones: 7300 W. Irving Pk. Rd. • Second Hand Tunes: 800 Dempster, Evanston*

9 Art & Antiques
For information on art exhibitions, get a copy of *Chicago Gallery News*, which is available at visitor centers, or head to the River North Gallery District *(see p77)*. Taylor's *Guide to Antique Shops in Illinois and Southern Wisconsin* (available in bookstores or by calling 1-847-465-3314) will direct you to the best local antique dealers.

10 Size Conversions
Clothing and shoe sizes in the UK, Europe, and the US differ, and conversions are complicated. Try *www.online conversion.com* for help.

Left **Continental Breakfast, Chicago style** Right **Pizzeria Uno**

TOP 10 Accommodation & Dining Tips

1 Booking a Room
To book a room, contact the Chicago Convention and Tourism Bureau (CCVB). Discounted rates *(see below)* can be found by checking the Internet on sites such as *www.877chicago.com*, calling the hotel directly, or contacting a reputable, no-fee reservation service such as Hot Rooms and Hotel Reservations Network. To hold a reservation, a credit card is usually necessary: no-shows will be charged. Be sure to specify if you want a smoking or non-smoking room.
Ⓢ *CCVB: 1-877-244-2246, www. choosechicago.com • Hot Rooms: 1-800-468-3500, www.hotrooms.com*

2 Rates
Hotel rates vary according to the hotel category, and the time of week and season. Peak rates are weekdays and from April–December. Rack rates, the basic room rates, are the ones used in this book to provide a guide price. Don't settle for them! It is almost always possible to get a better deal, so don't be too shy to ask.

3 Rooms
Usually, the larger the room, the higher the tab, and many, though not all, hotels charge more for a room with a view – so consider how much time you will want to spend in your room

before you pay the premium. Twin-bedded rooms are uncommon; most double rooms have either a queen- or king-sized bed or two double beds. If staying in a busy area, check to make sure rooms are soundproof.

4 Bed & Breakfasts
Bed & Breakfasts are a great way to see the city from a different perspective. For a list of homes offering guest rooms, check with At Home Inn Chicago, or Illinois Bed & Breakfast Association (ILBBA). Many require a minimum stay of two nights. Ⓢ *At Home Inn Chicago: 1-312-640-1050, 800-375-7084 (toll free) • www.athomeinnchicago.com • ILBBA: 1-888-523-2406 • www.bbonline.com*

5 Taxes
Downtown restaurants add on a 9.5 percent local sales tax to your check, and hotel tax in Chicago is quite high at 14.9 percent (though the suburbs are slightly cheaper). Room rates tend to be quoted without tax.

6 Restaurant Reservations
Some restaurants do not take reservations (or only for groups of more than five), while for others, in particular the upscale ones, reservations well in advance are a must, especially on weekends. We indicate a recommendation for the

restaurants listed in this book, but it is always a good idea to call and check, especially if you have special needs or dietary requirements.

7 Meal Times
Breakfast is usually served in diners and coffee shops from about 6–10am. Lunch is normally available from 11:30am–2pm, and dinner takes place between approximately 5–10pm depending on the establishment. Early-bird dinners, normally served from 5–7pm, are usually a good bargain.

8 Chicago-Style & Ethnic Cuisine
Deep-dish pizza, hot dogs, and steaks are Chicago's main specialties. But in a city where a multitude of cultures meet, so do a multitude of cuisines, so check out the city's many ethnic restaurants (see p42–3).

9 Portions
You will find that portions vary hugely from place to place. Often portions at upscale restaurants are smaller, while steakhouses and ethnic eateries offer a more than generous serving.

10 Dress Codes
Few restaurants have strict dress codes, though some hotel and other upscale restaurants still expect men to wear jackets and ties.

Price Categories

For a standard, double room per night (with breakfast if included), taxes and extra charges.

$	under $100
$$	$100–200
$$$	$200–300
$$$$	$300–400
$$$$$	over $400

Peninsula Chicago

🔟 Luxury Hotels

1 Ritz-Carlton
The Ritz has it all – superior service, an award-winning dining room, spa, and state-of-the-art-business facilities. Impressive views complement the classic furnishings and fine art in its spacious guest rooms, but it's the little things, like Bulgari toiletries and toys and cookies for the kids that puts it in a league of its own. 🔊 *160 E. Pearson St.* • *Map L2* • *312-266-1000* • *www.fourseasons.com* • *$$$$$*

2 Four Seasons
Expect the best in this grand hotel – possibly Chicago's most elegant. Lavish rooms command sweeping city and lake views, and chef Robert Sulatycky makes the award-winning Seasons restaurant a must try. 🔊 *120 E. Delaware Pl.* • *Map K2* • *312-280-8800* • *www.fourseasons.com* • *$$$$$*

3 Peninsula Chicago
Understated elegance sums up this hotel. Large, earth-toned rooms have dressing areas, and a steam-free TV screen and hands-free telephone is found in every bathroom. Floor-to-ceiling windows dramatize the lobby, where afternoon tea is accompanied by live classical music. 🔊 *108 E. Superior St.* • *Map L2* • *312-337-2888* • *http://fasttrack.chicago.peninsula.com* • *$$$$$*

4 The Drake
Popular with visiting celebrities and royalty, this is the grande dame of Chicago hotels, which effortlessly blends modern convenience with the charm of days gone by. Each of the 535 tastefully decorated rooms and suites is unique: many offer breathtaking views. 🔊 *140 E. Walton Pl.* • *Map L2* • *312-787-2200* • *www.thedrakehotel.com* • *$$$–$$$$$*

5 Sofitel Chicago Water Tower
This sleek, striking, ultra-modern hotel opened in 2003. Spectacular views, sumptuous feather beds, and private baths and showers feature in every room. 🔊 *20 E. Chestnut St.* • *Map K2* • *312-324-4000* • *www. sofitel.com* • *$$$–$$$$$*

6 Park Hyatt
Original contemporary art, rich woods, and warm tones create comfortable and tranquil public and private areas at this elegant boutiqe hotel. The state-of-the-art rooms feature furniture designed by Mies van der Rohe. 🔊 *800 N. Michigan Ave.* • *Map L2* • *312-335-1234* • *www.park chicago.hyatt.com* • *$$$$*

7 Fairmont
Overlooking Grant Park and Lake Michigan, the Fairmont features large, comfortably furnished rooms that include dressing areas and marble bathrooms. 🔊 *200 N. Columbus Dr.* • *Map L4* • *312-565-8000* • *www. fairmont.com* • *$$–$$$$$*

8 Renaissance Chicago Hotel
On the south bank of the Chicago River, this 27-story hotel affords amazing city views. Inviting guest rooms feature muted colors and warm woods, and the staff graciously accommodates all guests, even the four-legged ones. 🔊 *1 W. Wacker Dr.* • *Map K3* • *312-372-7200* • *www.renais sancehotels.com* • *$$$$*

9 InterContinental Chicago
One of the city's most luxurious hotels, which mixes historic charm with contemporary elegance. This former men's club *(see p27)* has stunning public rooms, and very comfortable guest rooms. 🔊 *505 N. Michigan Ave.* • *Map L2* • *312-944-4100* • *www.chicago.inter continental.com* • *$$$$*

10 Le Meridien
The interior opulence of this hotel, located on hip Rush Street, is undeniable. Contemporary rooms have beds with down comforters, and granite bathrooms with wall-to-wall mirrors. Public areas include a lovely terrace. 🔊 *521 N. Rush St.* • *Map L2* • *312-645-1500* • *www.lemeridien hotels.com* • *$$$*

Unless otherwise stated, all hotels accept credit cards, have private bathrooms, air con, non-smoking rooms, and rooms with DA

Left **The Hilton Chicago** Right **Guest room, Hotel Burnham**

Historic Hotels

1 The Hilton Chicago
When it opened in 1927, The Hilton was the world's largest hotel. Popular with many former US presidents, it oozes opulence, especially the Versailles-inspired Grand Ballroom. The Executive Class King Lakeview rooms offer the best views. ◎ *720 S. Michigan Ave. • Map L6 • 312-922-4400 • www. chicagohilton.com • $$$*

2 Palmer House Hilton
Palmer House has been an elegant fixture in the heart of the Loop for over 125 years. Extravagant frescoes decorate the ornate lobby's ceiling, while the guest rooms are subtly elegant. The hotel even has its own upscale shopping arcade. ◎ *17 E. Monroe St. • Map L4 • 312-726-7500 • www. chicagohilton.com • $$$*

3 Hotel Burnham
The Reliance Building – a handsome example of the Chicago School of architecture *(see p36–7)* – was reborn as the boutique Hotel Burnham in 1999. Plush rooms are decorated in gold and blue; some offer great views. ◎ *1 W. Washington St. • Map J4 • 312-782-1111 • www. burnhamhotel.com • $$–$$$*

4 Omni Ambassador East
In its heyday, this lavish hotel hosted stars such as Frank Sinatra and Liza Minelli. Comfortable rooms sport dark wood furniture and chintz furnishings; public areas are more impressive. ◎ *1301 N. State Pkwy. • Off map • 312-787-7200 • www. omnihotels.com • $$*

5 The Talbott
Enjoy the quiet elegance of this small, family-owned, European-style hotel. The Victorian parlor-like lobby and atmospheric Basil's bar and café offer a chance to unwind, and the 149 guest rooms and suites are large and welcoming. ◎ *20 E. Delaware Pl. • Map K2 • 312-944-4970 • www. talbotthotel.com • $$$*

6 Allerton Crowne Plaza
Originally a residential hotel, the Allerton Crowne has a high-ceilinged, 1940s-inspired lobby, and large, traditional guest rooms with marble baths and lots of amenities. Don't miss the panorama from the 25th floor. ◎ *701 N. Michigan Ave. • Map L2 • 312-440-1500 • www.sixcontinentshotels.com • $$–$$$*

7 The Whitehall
A quiet, understated European ambience has permeated this hotel since it opened in 1928. The 221 guest rooms combine elegant tradition with mod cons, and the Presidential Suite was a favorite of Katherine Hepburn. Check out the Molive restaurant with its menu of over 200 tantalizing martinis. ◎ *105 E. Delaware Pl. • Map K2 • 312-944-6300 • www.whitehallhotel.com • $$–$$$*

8 The Raphael
This former nurses' residence, built in the 1920s, now aptly bills itself as a quaint little hotel with old-world charm. The general effect is light and spacious, though some of the rooms and furnishings are a little tired. ◎ *201 E. Delaware Pl. • Map K2 • 312-943-5000 • www.raphaelchicago. com • $$$*

9 The Tremont
An inviting fireplace welcomes you at this 1920s-built hotel, where guest rooms are small but comfortable; some have antique furniture and four-posters. Mike Ditka's restaurant is famous for its steaks and the collection of sports memorabilia. ◎ *100 E. Chestnut St. • Map K2 • 312-751-1900 • www. tremontchicago.com • $$*

10 Millennium Knickerbocker
This hotel, once owned by Playboy Magazine, has hosted guests as famous as John Kennedy and Al Capone. Its 1930s lobby hosts the Martini Bar, and the guest rooms exude a timeless elegance. ◎ *163 E. Walton Pl. • Map L2 • 312-751-8100 • www. millenniumhotels.com • $$$*

Price Categories

For a standard,	
double room per	**$** under $100
night (with breakfast	**$$** $100–200
if included), taxes	**$$$** $200–300
and extra charges.	**$$$$** $300–400
	$$$$$ over $400

Left **Garden, Gold Coast Guest House B&B** Right **Wheeler Mansion**

Stylish Stays

1 W Chicago Lakeshore

A Zen water wall and "Leave me alone", rather than "Do not disturb" signs are indications of the W's hipper take on the hotel experience. The modern guest rooms have lovely views, as does the rooftop lounge, Whiskey Sky (see p44). 🕲 644 N. Lake Shore Dr. • Map M3 • 312-943-9200 • www.whotels.com • $$$

2 Wheeler Mansion

An immaculate 11-room hotel, this 130-year-old mansion is known for its great attention to detail. Soak up the lavish artwork, period features, and antique furniture, or take it easy in the tranquil garden. 🕲 2020 S. Calumet Ave. • Off map • 312-945-2020 • www.wheeler mansion.com • $$$–$$$$

3 House of Blues Hotel

This amazing hotel is much more than just somewhere to lay your head. A golden Buddha welcomes guests, and the atmospheric Kaz Bar has a Moroccan theme. State-of-the-art rooms offer hi-tech entertainment and eclectic decor. 🕲 333 N. Dearborn St. • Map K3 • 312-245-0333 • www.houseofblues.com • $$

4 W Chicago City Center

This hotel is trendy yet traditional, with comfy couches and board games in the lobby. Guest room decor is inspired by 1940s Hollywood glamor, with chaises longues and ostrich-leather headboards. 🕲 172 W. Adams St. • Map J4 • 312-332-1200 • www.whotels.com • $$$–$$$$

5 Hotel Monaco

Most of the luxe rooms in this stylish 14-story hotel feature window seats (a.k.a "secluded meditation stations"), while the spirit is further calmed by aromatherapy oils in the bathrooms. Pep things up in the Party Like a Rock Star Suite, complete with jukebox and Jacuzzi tub. 🕲 225 N. Wabash Ave. • Map K3 • 312- 960-8500 • www.monaco-chicago.com • $$

6 The Blake Hotel at Printers Row

This hotel contained printing presses before ever housing people. Now a National Historic Landmark, it offers large, light rooms. Savor Midwestern delicacies at the award-winning Prairie restaurant. 🕲 500 S. Dearborn St. • Map K5 • 312-986-1234 • www.printersrow.hyatt.com • $$$

7 Crowne Plaza Silversmith

Built in 1897, this beautiful building incorporates both Romanesque Revival and Arts and Crafts styles. The large guest rooms have Frank Lloyd Wright-inspired furniture, high ceilings, and large windows – though views (of the El tracks) are only worthwhile from the fifth floor and above. 🕲 10 S. Wabash Ave. • Map K4 • 312-372-7696 • www.crowneplaza.com • $$$

8 Hard Rock Hotel

This extravagant 381-room, musically themed hotel occupies the former Carbide and Carbon building – an Art Deco creation of 1929. Piped music and memorabilia are everywhere, and rooms are stylish but fun. 🕲 230 N. Michigan Ave. • Map L2 • 312-345-1000 • www.hardrock.com • $$$

9 Hotel Allegro

Here, designer Cheryl Rowley has combined classic Art Deco features with contemporary colors and textures to great effect at this musically themed hotel. Complimentary coffee and wine are standard. Fresh and fun. 🕲 171 W. Randolph St. • Map J4 • 312-236-0123 • www.hotelallegro chicago.com • $$

10 Gold Coast Guest House B&B

This 1873 town house makes a pleasant change from the large hotels, with just four individually decorated rooms. Guests are welcome to use the comfortable sitting room and ivy-walled garden. 🕲 113 W. Elm St. • Map K1 • 312-337-0361 • www.bbchicago.com • No DA • $$

Left **Homewood Suites** Right **Lobby, Hilton Garden Inn**

Budget Sleeps

1 Best Western Hawthorne Terrace

Warm and inviting sums up this 59-room hotel. An outdoor terrace overlooks the Lake View area, and guests can also use a small exercise room with sauna and whirlpool. Continental breakfast is included. ✪ *3434 N. Broadway • Map E2 • 1-773-244-3434 • www.hawthorne terrace.com • $$–$$$*

2 Days Inn Lincoln Park North

This hotel is Chicago's highest-rated Days Inn. Free passes to the fitness center next door are part of the deal when you stay here. Guest rooms include facilities such as microwaves and refrigerators. ✪ *644 W. Diversey Pkwy. • Map E2 • 1-773-525-7010 • www.lpndaysinn.com • $$*

3 Fitzpatrick Chicago

Experience a little bit of the Emerald Isle here, with Fitzer's Irish Pub and an all-day Irish breakfast. A Waterford crystal chandelier hangs in the lobby, and Celtic motifs appear throughout. The rooftop pool provides great views of the city. ✪ *166 E. Superior St. • Map L2 • 312-787-6000 • www.fitzpatrick hotels.com • $$*

4 Embassy Suites Chicago: Downtown Lakefront

The impressive 13-story Sky Lobby offers a great place to unwind, with its soaring atrium. Glass-sided elevators whisk guests to suites with amenities that include high-speed Internet access and microwaves. Full American breakfast is also included. ✪ *511 N. Columbus Dr. • Map L4 • 1-888-903-8884 • www. chicagoembassy.com • $$$*

5 The Inn at Lincoln Park

This hotel's Tudor-style exterior, Victorian lobby, and wagon-wheel trim are best described as eclectic. And while the rooms are definitely no-frills, the complimentary breakfast and exercise room are real draws. ✪ *601 W. Diversey Pkwy. • Map E2 • 1-773-348-2810 • $$*

6 Homewood Suites by Hilton

The two-room suites in this great value hotel all have fully equipped kitchens, as well as living rooms with extra queen-size sofa beds. Use of the 19th-floor indoor pool and the fitness center all add to your stay here. ✪ *40 E. Grand Ave. • Map L3 • 312-644-2222 • www.home woodsuiteschicago.com • $$*

7 Hilton Garden Inn

Each of this hotel's functional and spacious 357 rooms offers a large desk, complimentary high speed Internet access, hospitality center, and many other amenities. Six corner suites offer the perfect setup for families and groups of friends: the hotel also has a pool and gym. ✪ *10 E .Grand Ave. • Map L3 • 312-595-0000 • www.hiltongarden inn.com • $$$*

8 Hampton Inn & Suites

This centrally located, family-friendly hotel offers two-room suites – with fully equipped kitchens – as well as many standard guest rooms. Bonuses include the fitness facility, indoor pool, complimentary breakfast buffet, and daily newspaper. ✪ *33 W. Illinois St. • Map K3 • 312-832-0330 • www. hamptoninn.com • $$*

9 Red Roof Inn Chicago

This is a great option for budget-minded travelers. Rooms at this centrally located inn are small, but they have all the essentials. A branch of the Coco Pazzo restaurant chain is on site. ✪ *162 E. Ontario St. • Map L2 • 312-787-3580 • www.redroof.com • $$*

10 Hostelling International Chicago

This place is great value if you don't mind sleeping in a basic dormitory with local students, and paying a small yearly membership fee. The facility includes lounges, fully equipped kitchens, and bed linen. ✪ *24 E. Congress Pkwy. • Map L5 • 312-360-0300 • www.hi-chicago.org • $*

Some budget accommodations offer weekday evening receptions with complimentary refreshments.

Price Categories

For a standard, double room per night (with breakfast if included), taxes and extra charges.

$	under $100
$$	$100–200
$$$	$200–300
$$$$	$300–400
$$$$$	over $400

View of Atrium, Embassy Suites Chicago Downtown

🔟 Business-Friendly Stays

1 Sheraton Chicago Hotel & Towers

The large, stylish guest rooms here offer fantastic lake, city, or river views. The hotel also has its own business center, boat dock, health club, and five restaurants. Popular with conventioneers. ◎ 301 N. Water St. • Off map • 312-464-1000 • www.sheraton chicago.com • $$$

2 Westin Chicago River North

This sleek, four-star venue is home to a state-of-the-art Executive Business Center, fitness facility, and guest rooms featuring the ultra-comfortable Westin Heavenly Bed. ◎ 320 N. Dearborn Ave. • Map K3 • 312-744-1900 • www. westinrivernorth.com • $$$

3 Hyatt Regency McCormick Place

Linked by a connecting walkway to McCormick Place convention center, the basic but modern rooms of the 32-story Hyatt Regency are an attractive stopover for conventioneers. The hotel also has a fitness facility. ◎ 2233 S. Martin Luther King Dr. • Map D5 • 312-567-1234 • www.mccormick place.hyatt.com • $$

4 Embassy Suites Hotel O'Hare-Rosemont

This hotel's seven-story garden atrium makes a pleasant retreat from the hustle and bustle of the nearby convention center and airport. Suites have all the necessary facilities; cooked breakfasts and an airport shuttle are complimentary. ◎ 5500 N. River Rd., Rosemont • Off map • 1-847-678-4000 • www. embassyohare.com • $$$

5 Swissôtel

Rising up where the Chicago River and Lake Michigan meet is this dramatic glass-and-steel creation. Oversized guest rooms contain every convenience for the business traveller and provide stellar views of the city. ◎ 323 E. Wacker Dr. • Map L3 • 312-565-0565 • www. swissotel.com • $$$

6 Hyatt Regency Chicago

A lobby full of greenery and fountains welcomes guests into this, the biggest hotel in the Hyatt chain. Although all guest rooms offer high speed Internet access, you can opt for a "Business Plan" upgrade to obtain more specific benefits during your stay. ◎ 151 E. Wacker Dr. • Map L3 • 312-565-1234 • www. hyatt.com • $$$–$$$$

7 Chicago Marriott Downtown

This 46-story hotel's contemporary rooms are designed to cater to every business need. Guests can enjoy the hotel's five restaurants and lounges, or its on-site pool and fitness center. ◎ 540 N. Michigan Ave. • Map L2 • 312-836-0100 • www.marriott.com • $$$

8 Embassy Suites Hotel Chicago Downtown

The lofty atrium here is filled with plants, birds, and fountains; the two-room suites are spacious and well-equipped; service is personal; and cooked breakfasts plus other perks are included. ◎ 600 N. State St. • Map K2 • 312-943-3800 • www. embassysuites.com • $$

9 Courtyard by Marriott Chicago Downtown

Bright, modern rooms with high speed Internet access, a spacious work area, and an extra sofa-bed make this centrally located hotel a popular choice among leisure and business travelers alike. ◎ 30 E. Hubbard St. • Map K3 • 312-329-2500 • www. courtyard.com • $$

10 Hilton Chicago O'Hare Airport

The only hotel actually on airport grounds (conveniently linked to airport terminals via underground walkways) offers an enhanced business center, providing state-of-the-art telecommunications and multimedia conference facilities. Rooms are well soundproofed. ◎ O'Hare Airport • Map A3 • 1-773-686-8000 • www.hilton.com • $$$

> Unless otherwise stated, all hotels accept credit cards, have private bathrooms, air con, non-smoking rooms, and rooms with DA

General Index

Acknowledgements

The Authors
Chicago-based freelancer Elaine Glusac specializes in travel writing for an array of publications including *National Geographic Traveler* and the *International Herald Tribune*.

Elisa Kronish is a Chicago native who has written about the city's highlights and hidden finds for a variety of print and online travel guides such as Citysearch Chicago.

Roberta Sotonoff is a travel junkie. She writes about a variety of travel destinations, and her work has appeared worldwide in over 40 newspapers, magazines, on-line sites and guidebooks.

Produced by Departure Lounge, London
Editorial Director Naomi Peck
Art Director Lisa Kosky
Picture Researcher Debbie Woska
Editorial and Design Assistance Kelly Thompson, Davin Kuntze, Debbie Woska, Caroline Blake
Photographer Jim Warych
Additional Photography Andrew Leyerle
Illustrator Lee Redmond
Maps (DK India) Managing Editor: Aruna Ghose, Senior Cartographer: Uma Bhattacharya, Cartographers: Suresh Kumar, Alok Pathak
Proofreader Mary Sutherland
Factchecker Misty Tosh
Indexer Hilary Bird

AT DORLING KINDERSLEY
Publishing Managers Fay Franklin, Kate Poole
Senior Art Editor Marisa Renzullo
Publisher Douglas Amrine
Senior Cartographic Editor Casper Morris
DTP Jason Little, Conrad van Dyk

Production Controller Shane Higgins
Additional Contributions D Clancy Marianne Petrou, Brett Steel, Ros Walford

Picture Credits
t-top; tl-top left; tlc-top left centre; tc-top centre; tr-top right; cla-centre left above; ca-centre above; cra-centre right above; cl-centre left; c-centre; cr-centre right; clb-centre left below; cb-centre below; crb-centre right below; bl-bottom left, b-bottom; bc-bottom centre; bcl-bottom centre left; br-bottom right; d-detail.

Every effort has been made to trace the copyright holders, and we apologize for any unintentional omissions. We would be pleased to insert the appropriate acknowledgements in any subsequent editions of this publication.

The publishers would like to thank the following individuals, companies and picture libraries for their kind permission to reproduce their photographs.

20th CENTURY FOX: 61tr
ALAMY: 4–5 (Edward Hattersley); 31tl (Arcaid Ed); 32–33 (Jason Lindsey); 34c (Popperfoto); 66–67 (Andre Jenny); 37d (Popperfoto)
ALAN KLEHR: 14–15c; 76–77
ART INSTITUTE OF CHICAGO: 6cra; 8cb; 9c; 2tl, 9tl; 9cra; 9bl; *American Gothic* by Grant Wood. Friends of the American Art Collection. All rights reserved by Art Institute of Chicago and VAGA, New York, NY and DACS London, 2005. 10tl North American, New Mexico, Mimbres, Salado Region. Ritual Cache Figure; 10tc Tennessee, Entrance Hall, 1835, 'Thorne Miniature Room'; 10tr Panel (detail) of butterflies, 1850s, 19th century England; 10 bl; 11tr